Home Team Advantage
A Sole Proprietorship Merchandise Business

INCLUDES:
- Company Profile
- Your Role as Accountant
- Daily Procedures
- Weekly Procedures
- Monthly Procedures
- End-of-Year Procedures
- Accounting Forms
- Managerial Analysis Questions

Price ▪ Haddock ▪ Brock

McGraw-Hill Irwin

Boston   Burr Ridge, IL   Dubuque, IA   Madison, WI   New York   San Francisco   St. Louis
Bangkok   Bogotá   Caracas   Kuala Lumpur   Lisbon   London   Madrid   Mexico City
Milan   Montreal   New Delhi   Santiago   Seoul   Singapore   Sydney   Taipei   Toronto

McGraw-Hill Irwin

HOME TEAM ADVANTAGE: A SOLE PROPRIETORSHIP MERCHANDISE BUSINESS
John Price, M. David Haddock, and Horace Brock

Published by McGraw-Hill/Irwin, an imprint of The McGraw-Hill Companies, Inc., 1221 Avenue of the Americas, New York, NY 10020. Copyright © 2007 by The McGraw-Hill Companies, Inc. All rights reserved.

1 2 3 4 5 6 7 8 9 0 QPD/QPD 0 9 8 7 6

ISBN-13: 978-0-07-319685-5
ISBN-10: 0-07-319685-1

www.mhhe.com

The McGraw-Hill Companies

Table of Contents

INTRODUCTION TO THE BUSINESS

BACKGROUND

Home Team Advantage is a retailer of sports memorabilia. The business is a sole proprietorship owned by Dan Morris, who started it twelve years after a career as a local television sports announcer. At the end of his contract, and after a long run in the Dallas area as a recognizable sports announcer for two local stations, Morris was offered a post in a smaller market, out of Texas. Morris' other option was to remain in the Dallas area-the community to which he reported for over a decade-and follow his passion for sports. Hence, he realized the dream of Home Team Advantage, which he runs with his son Ron.

LOCATION

Twenty minutes east of Dallas, Texas, Grand Prairie is on the main route to Fort Worth. Directly across Tyler Avenue from the Grand Prairie Mall, Home Team Advantage has ample free parking. Also, because of the multiplex movie theaters and restaurants, plenty of evening foot traffic justifies maintaining a nine o'clock dosing hour.

FACILITIES AND LAYOUT

The one-story, company-owned building, is arranged in three sections: the Game Room, the Hall of Fame, and the Winner's Circle. The front entrance brings a visitor into the main area which occupies two thirds of the store-the Game Room. Here, poster-sized color photos of famous sports moments adorn the colorfully appointed store. A big screen TV plays recent sports coverage. This is where sports fans will find sports T-shirts, caps and sports jerseys, sweatshirts and collectibles. New special event displays every month guarantee a fresh feeling for return customers.

The Hall of Fame is located off the Game Room through double hardwood doors. Collectors are attracted through these doors to the renowned collection of sports treasures. Various items are mounted on the wall, under tasteful track lighting, some for display only, others for sale: a signed Babe Ruth bat, a famous home run baseball, a signed Super Bowl football, and a baseball program from the 1926 World Series, etc. In another Hall of Fame niche, a video is always running of one of the Olympic games — next to the vast Olympic display of photos, authentic uniforms, medals, and pins. Found in another section of the Hall of Fame is a bounty of trading cards. Various hardwood bookshelves hold the latest sports books as well as rare out-of-print editions.

The Hall of Fame is also something of a shrine to the career of Dan Morris. Many black and white photos picturing Dan and a variety of sports icons adorn the walls of this museum-like room. The heart and soul of Home Team Advantage, the Hall of Fame, is the main attraction of the store.

The Winner's Circle can be adapted for a variety of uses. It can be utilized for visiting sports stars and autograph signing, or it can display special sporting event related merchandise. Clients have used the Winner's Circle to host small meetings and to screen sporting event tapings. Dan places a high value on his community involvement, and he offers the area as a gathering spot for Little League teams whose uniforms he has sponsored. He's also hosted a few announcements of new memorabilia acquisitions from the colorful Winner's Circle area.

PERSONNEL

Home Team Advantage is managed by Dan Morris, the owner, and has a staff of nine full-time employees. This includes the position of accountant, for which you have just been hired.

TABLE 1 EMPLOYEES

NAME	TITLE	DUTIES
Dan Morris	Owner and Manager	Manages store operations and supervises the entire staff. Authorizes all orders for new merchandise, and makes pricing decisions when merchandise arrives. Verifies all invoices prior to payment, and signs all checks. Responsible for staff training. Handles customer service problems and problems with suppliers.
Karen King	Sales Supervisor and Assistant Manager	Supervises other salespersons and does some selling. Serves as assistant manager when Dan Morris is away from the store.
Ron Morris	Special Sales Representative	Responsible for sales in the Hall of Fame Travels to sporting contests and conventions.
Amanda Sorenson	Salesperson	Responsible for sales in the Game Room.
Janetha Johnson	Salesperson	Responsible for sales in the Game Room.
Sam Kano	Salesperson	Responsible for sales in the Hall of Fame.
Arturo Cortez	Stockroom Supervisor	Manages the stockroom. Inspects new merchandise, and prepares receiving reports. Arranges for the pricing and transfer of merchandise to sales areas and for deliveries to customers. Keeps stockroom records. Supervises the stockroom clerk.
Danny Silvestri	Stockroom Clerk	Assists the stockroom supervisor. Unpacks new merchandise, prepares merchandise for delivery to customer, and drives the delivery van.
Joanna Wilson	Cashier	Receives cash from customers and processes all charge account and bank credit card sales. Prepares the daily bank deposit and takes it to the bank. Handles the petty cash fund. Responsible for running the computer programs and providing a daily cash register summary and a daily inventory update.
You	Accountant	Maintains accounting records and files. Prepares financial statements and special reports as requested by the owner. Issues checks to pay bills and maintains the checkbook. Reconciles the monthly bank statement. Assists the store's outside accounting firm with the annual audit.

Figure 1

HOME TEAM ADVANTAGE
Organization Chart

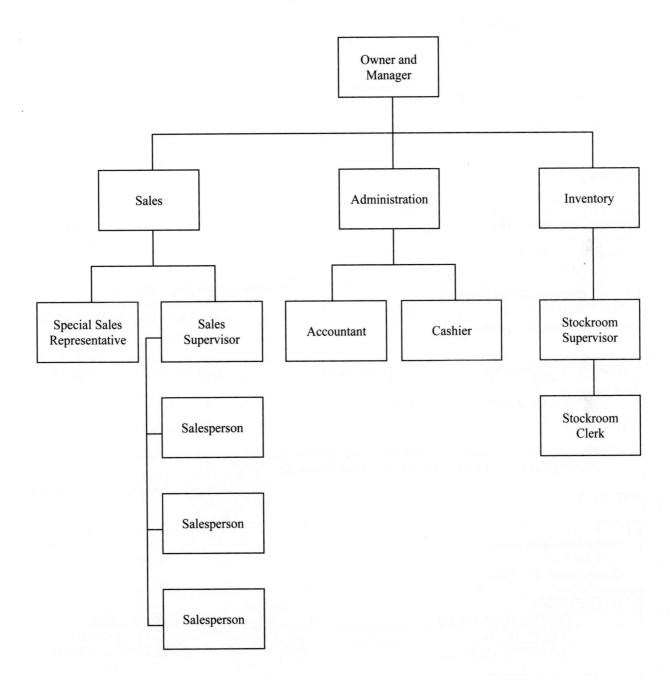

COMPANY PROCEDURES

The basic procedures that Home Team Advantage uses to carry on daily business activities are described in this section.

PURCHASING PROCEDURES

The purchasing procedures are as follows:

(1) Home Team Advantage utilizes the periodic inventory system. The cashier inspects merchandise on hand regularly, and notifies the owner which items must be ordered.

(2) The owner issues a purchase order to the manufacturer or wholesaler that handles the item. (See Figure 2.)

FIGURE 2

Home Team Advantage 201 Tyler Ave. Grand Prairie, TX 75050					Purchase Order

TO	Calderon Sports Supply 7923 W. 16th St. Indianapolis, IN 46222		Purchase Order No.: 664 Date: November 18, 20-- Ship Via: Fort Pitt Trucking Co. Terms: 5/10, n30		

Quantity	Catalog No.	Description	Unit Price	Amount
50	8-2468-21	Die-Cast Cars	$ 5.00	$ 250.00

(3) When the merchandise arrives, the stockroom clerk unpacks it, and the stockroom supervisor inspects it and fills out a receiving report. (See Figure 3.)

FIGURE 3

Home Team Advantage 201 Tyler Ave. Grand Prairie, TX 75050			

RECEIVED FROM:

Calderon Sports Supply 7923 W. 16th St. Indianapolis, IN 46222			DATE RECEIVED: 11/19/20-- PURCHASE ORDER NO.: 664

SHIPPER For Pitt Trucking Co.		SHIPPED VIA Truck	ACCEPTED BY AC

QUANTITY RECEIVED	QUANITY ACCEPTED	CATALOG NO.	DECRIPTION
50	50	8-2468-21	Die-Cast Cars

Home Team Advantage Practice Set

(4) The owner prices the merchandise, and the stockroom supervisor attaches price tags to the individual items.

(5) The stockroom clerk moves the merchandise to the designated area in the stockroom or to the appropriate sales area.

SALES PROCEDURES

The sales procedures are as follows:

(1) A salesperson helps the customer select merchandise and prepares a sales slip for the transaction.

(2) The customer takes the sales slip to the store's cashier and either pays for the goods in cash, uses a bank credit card, or uses a credit card issued by Home Team Advantage.

(3) The cashier records the sale using the store's cash register. Home Team Advantage has an electronic cash register system that uses a "store and forward" system. As individual transactions are entered each day, this system stores data about transactions on a magnetic disk. At the end of the day, the disk is removed from the register and placed in the computer for processing. Thus, data is "forwarded" from the cash register system to the computer system. During the day, whenever a sale occurs, the cashier places the sales slip in a slot in the cash register and then records the following data about the sale: type of sale-cash, bank credit card, or charge account; customer number for a charge account sale; quantity and type of merchandise; and unit price. The cash register automatically extends the price and computes the sales tax and total price. This data, along with a description of the items sold, is printed on the sales slip by the cash register.

   (a) *Cash sales.* If the sale is for cash, the cashier will complete the transaction by collecting the cash and giving the customer a copy of the sales slip as a receipt.

   (b) *Bank credit card sales.* If the customer uses a bank credit card, credit authorization must be obtained before completing the transaction. The cashier passes the customer's card through a slot at the *back* of a small machine and enters the amount of the sale on the keyboard of the machine. This machine is connected electronically through a telephone line to the bank's credit card authorization department. An "electronic authorization" is relayed to the store's machine if the sale is acceptable. If it is, the cashier completes the transaction by using the customer's credit card to imprint the name and account number on a special credit card sales slip and by having the customer sign the sales slip. A copy of this sales slip and a copy of the store's own sales slip are given to the customer as a record of the transaction.

   (c) *Charge account sales.* If the customer is using a Home Team Advantage credit card, the cashier will check the files to be sure the customer has a satisfactory credit standing. For sales over $500, the cashier must also obtain the owner's authorization before completing the sale. After verifying the customer's credit status, the cashier uses the customer's Home Team Advantage credit card to imprint the name and account number on the sales slip, has the customer sign the slip, and gives the customer a copy of the slip as a receipt.

(4) If the customer requests home delivery, the cashier enters the necessary information on the sales slip and gives a copy to the stockroom supervisor, who arranges to have the stockroom clerk package and deliver the merchandise.

(5) During the day, the cashier also uses the cash register to record cash collected from customers in settlement of their charge account balances. These amounts are received from the customers by mail and in person.

(6) At the end of the day, the cashier removes the magnetic disk from the cash register and inserts it in the disk drive of the office computer. The disk drive is able to "read" the data stored on the disk. This data is then combined with file data from another disk and is processed by the computer system to produce a daily cash register summary.

The cash register summary lists all information about cash receipts in one section and all information about charge account sales in another section, as shown in Figure 4. Notice that there are three sources of cash receipts-cash sales, bank credit card sales, and collections on accounts receivable. The bank credit card sales are considered a source of cash receipts because the sales slips from these sales are taken to the bank with a special deposit slip each day, and the bank credits the total amount shown on the sales slips to the store's checking account as if it were a cash deposit. (At the end of the month, the bank deducts a fee for handling the credit card sales. This fee appears on the monthly bank statement that the firm receives.)

FIGURE 4

CASH REGISTER SUMMARY

CASH COLLECTIONS 12/01/20--

CUSTOMER NO.	SOURCE	ACCTS. REC. COLLECTED	AMOUNT OF SALE	SALES TAX	CASH RECEIVED
	Cash Sales		577.51	46.20	623.71
	Bank Credit Card Sales		1,186.34	94.91	1,281.25
2369	Steve Carlyle	72.15			72.15
	TOTALS	72.15	1,763.85	141.11	1,977.11

CHARGE ACCOUNT SALES

CUSTOMER NO.	CUSTOMER NAME	AMOUNT OF SALE	SALES TAX	TOTAL RECEIVABLE
2984	Jamaal Howard	118.06	9.44	127.50
	TOTALS	118.06	9.44	127.50

(7) The magnetic disk taken from the cash register also contains data about the quantity and type of merchandise sold. The computer system uses this data to produce a daily summary of sales by item. A sample of a daily summary of sales by item is shown in Figure 5.

Home Team Advantage Practice Set

FIGURE 5

DAILY SUMMARY OF SALES BY ITEM		DATE: 11/20--
STOCK NO.	ITEM	QUANTITY SOLD
DCC12	Die-Cast Cars	25
BAJ15	Baseball Jerseys	50

YOUR ROLE AS AN ACCOUNTANT

ACCOUNTING RECORDS

For the past two years you have been studying accounting at a local college. Dan Morris has asked you to begin working on December 1, 20--, as the accountant for Home Team Advantage, reporting to him. You have accepted the position.

Upon arriving for work on Monday, December 1, 20--, you learn that the business has a fiscal year ending each December 31 and that your predecessor has journalized and posted all transactions through November 30 of the current fiscal year. You find that all records are up to date, were proved at the end of November, and are in good order. Dan Morris explains that you will have full responsibility for the checkbook, the five journals used, the general ledger, the subsidiary ledgers, and all other financial records and statements.

CASH PROCEDURES

Recording Bank Deposits. All cash (including currency, coins, checks, and money orders) that the firm receives is processed by the cashier and deposited daily. The special sales slips for the bank credit card sales are also deposited each day. The bank's discount fee for handling these transactions is automatically deducted from the business's checking account at the end of the month, and the amount deducted is shown on the monthly bank statement.

The cashier prepares two bank deposit slips – one for the cash processed through the cash register and one for the bank credit card sales slips. Occasionally, there will also be other types of cash receipts transactions that will require the preparation of a bank deposit slip. When the cashier returns from the bank, she will give you the validated deposit slips so that you can enter the necessary data in the cash receipts journal.

Issuing Checks. All expenditures of Home Team Advantage, except petty cash payments, are made by check. The checks are prepared by the owner and recorded by you.

CASH RECEIPTS JOURNAL

At the close of business each day, the cashier uses the computer system to produce a daily cash register summary. These cash register summaries are located on pages 25-56. You will record all the cash from cash sales, bank credit card sales, and accounts receivable collections in the cash receipts journal. Occasionally, there will also be other types of cash receipts transactions that must be entered in the cash receipts journal.

Credits to customers' accounts in the accounts receivable subsidiary ledger are posted daily from the cash receipts journal. Items in the Other Accounts Credit column of this journal are posted at the end of each week. Summary postings of all column totals (except the total of the Other Accounts Credit column) are made at the end of the month.

Use 35 as the first page number for the cash receipts journal when you begin making entries. (Pages 1-34 were used to record the previous months' transactions.)

CASH PAYMENTS JOURNAL

You should record all checks in the cash payments journal on a daily basis. Invoices and bills covering expenses are paid promptly upon receipt, and the transactions are entered in the cash payments journal immediately after the checks are prepared. Invoices covering purchases of merchandise for resale include a credit period and are therefore entered in the purchases journal when they are first received. These invoices are paid later in accordance with the credit terms, and the checks issued are then recorded in the cash payments journal. The cashier handles petty cash payments, which are periodically reimbursed by a check that you prepare. The amounts involved are recorded in the cash payments journal when the reimbursement check is issued.

Debits to creditors' accounts in the accounts payable subsidiary ledger are posted daily from the cash payments journal. Items in the Other Accounts Debit column of this journal are posted at the end of each week. Summary postings of all column totals (except the total of the Other Accounts Debit column) are made at the end of the month.

Use 35 as the first page number for the cash payments journal when you begin making entries. (Pages 1-34 were used to record previous months' transactions.)

SALES JOURNAL

The cashier records all charge account sales on the cash register. The cash register summary prepared by the computer system each day lists these sales and provides the information that you need to enter them in the sales journal. Charge account customers normally have **30** days in which to pay. Cash discounts are not granted.

Each day you should post from the sales journal to customers' accounts in the accounts receivable subsidiary ledger. You make monthly summary postings of the column totals to the appropriate accounts in the general ledger.

Use 35 as the first page number for the sales journal when you begin making entries. (Pages 1-34 were used to record previous months' transactions.)

PURCHASES JOURNAL

The owner verifies all invoices received from suppliers and then gives you the invoices to record. You enter the credit purchases of merchandise for resale in the purchases journal.

Each day you should post from the purchases journal to the creditors' accounts in the accounts payable subsidiary ledger. You make monthly summary postings of the column totals to the appropriate general ledger accounts.

Use 35 as the first page number for the purchases journal when you begin making entries. (Pages 1-34 were used to record previous months' transactions.)

GENERAL JOURNAL

Any transactions that cannot be recorded in the special journals are entered in the general journal. This journal is also used for adjusting, dosing, and reversing entries at the end of the fiscal year.

Post from the general journal at the end of the week. Use 35 as the first page number for the general journal when you begin making entries. (Pages 1-34 were used to record previous months' transactions.)

GENERAL LEDGER

Balance-form ledger sheets are used for the general ledger accounts. The previous accountant prepared a trial balance as of November 30 to check the equality of the debits and credits in these accounts. The December 1 balances have been entered for your convenience. The chart of accounts is reproduced on page 72 for easy reference. (Note: Some of the accounts show no balances as of December 1.)

SUBSIDIARY LEDGERS

Home Team Advantage has two subsidiary ledgers: an accounts receivable ledger and an accounts payable ledger.

Accounts Receivable Ledger. Accounts with individual customers are kept in alphabetical order on balance-form ledger sheets. The previous accountant proved this ledger against the Accounts Receivable account in the general ledger as of November 30. The December balances have been entered for your convenience. Postings to this ledger are made daily from the sales journal and the cash receipts journal, and weekly from the general journal.

Accounts Payable Ledger. Accounts with individual creditors are kept in alphabetical order using balance-form ledger sheets. The previous accountant proved this ledger against the Accounts Payable account in the general ledger as of November 30. The December 1 balances have been entered for your convenience. Postings to the accounts payable ledger are made daily from the purchases journal and the cash payments journal, and weekly from the general journal.

SUMMARY OF ROUTINE ACCOUNTING PROCEDURES

The routine accounting procedures that you must perform for Home Team Advantage during December are summarized below. The chart of accounts for the business appears on page 72.

DAILY PROCEDURES

The daily procedures include journalizing all transactions and posting appropriate entries to the subsidiary ledgers. Daily postings ensure that the balances in the subsidiary ledger accounts are always current. As previously noted, the balances as of December 1 have already been entered in the ledgers. You are to begin your work with the recording of transactions for the month of December.

PAYROLL PROCEDURES

The full-time employees of Home Team Advantage are paid semimonthly-on the 15th and on the last business day of each month. Home Team Advantage uses Payroll Systems Inc., an automated payroll service company, to handle most payroll functions. This company prepares the semimonthly payroll, prepares quarterly and year-end payroll tax returns, and keeps an individual earnings record for each employee. By using an outside service company to handle payroll work, Mr. Morris has more time to devote to the operations of his business. In addition, the service company guarantees the accuracy of the payroll and relieves Mr. Morris of the need to keep informed about changes in payroll tax rates and the requirements for filing payroll tax returns.

Payroll Systems Inc. has the name, address, marital status, number of withholding allowances, and hourly rate of each employee of Home Team Advantage. Shortly before each payday, Mr. Morris reports the number of hours worked by each employee during the pay period to Payroll Systems Inc. electronically. Payroll Systems Inc. then computes the gross earnings, deductions, and net pay for each employee; prepares a payroll register, a payroll summary, and payroll checks; and updates the employee earnings records. The company delivers the payroll register, summary, and checks the day before the employees are to be paid, and Mr. Morris reviews all the documents for accuracy. He then signs the checks and distributes them to the employees.

For ease in maintaining its bank records, Home Team Advantage uses a separate checking account just for payroll. Working from the payroll summary, you will issue a check from the regular checking account equal to the total net pay. This check will be deposited in the payroll account to cover the employees' individual paychecks. You will also use the payroll summary to journalize and post the accounting entries for payroll and payroll taxes.

END-OF-WEEK PROCEDURES
The routine procedures to be completed at the end of each week are outlined below.

(1) Foot the amount columns in the cash receipts, cash payments, sales, and purchases journals. Enter the footings in small pencil figures immediately beneath the last line on which an entry has been made. Cross-foot to prove the equality of the debit and credit footings.

(2) Post all individual entries from the general journal and from the Other Accounts columns of the cash receipts journal and the cash payments journal to the general ledger.

(3) Answer the Audit Check questions. Your instructor will indicate how you can determine the accuracy of your answers to these questions.

NARRATIVE OF TRANSACTIONS
The transactions that took place at Home Team Advantage during December 20-- are listed in this section. You are expected to record each transaction in the order given. Copies of the daily cash register summaries are given on pages 25-56. Refer to the appropriate summary form as necessary to complete your work. The other business papers that the accountant would normally receive are not included, but the essential data from them are given in the narrative of transactions. The journals, ledgers, working papers, and statement forms that you will need are provided on pages 57-112.

MONDAY, DECEMBER 1
Transaction 1   Issued Check 609 for $650 on account for an October invoice to Archival Card Storage Suppliers for cardholders, plaques, and acid-free boxes.

Transaction 2   Purchased basketball jerseys from Duong's Jersey Outlet for $12,058.50; terms net 30 days; Invoice 608 dated November 29.

Transaction 3   Received the daily cash register summary. Also received deposit slips totaling $1,977.11.

TUESDAY, DECEMBER 2

Transaction 4   Issued Check 610 for $524.79 to Department of Power for electricity used in the store for the month of November.

Transaction 5   Issued Check 611 for $2,500 to Grand Prairie Management for lease and property maintenance fees.

Transaction 6   Received the daily cash register summary. Also received deposit slips totaling $3,429.35.

WEDNESDAY, DECEMBER 3

Transaction 7   Purchased baseball bat display cases from Woodworks, Inc. for $750; terms 2/10, n/30; Invoice 2932 dated December 1.

Transaction 8   Issued Check 612 for $1,340 to Prism Insurance for the fire insurance policy premium.

Transaction 9   Received the daily cash register summary. Also received deposit slips totaling $3,423.52.

THURSDAY, DECEMBER 4

Transaction 10   Issued Check 613 for $300 to Tyler Disposal Services for rubbish removal.

Transaction 11   Issued Check 614 for $5,000 to Sports Authentica for signed Championship baseball jerseys for November invoices.

Transaction 12   Received the daily cash register summary. Also received deposit slips totaling $2,969.52.

FRIDAY, DECEMBER 5

Transaction 13   Issued Check 615 for $3,204 to First Bank of Texas for deposit of amounts withheld from employees' earnings for the semimonthly payroll period ended November 30 and employer's share of social security and Medicare tax as follows:

Social Security Tax Withheld	$541.00
Medicare Tax Withheld	126.00
Federal Income Tax Withheld	1,870.00
Social Security Tax – Employer's Share	541.00
Medicare Tax – Employer's Share	126.00

Transaction 14   Issued Check 616 to Dallas Telephone for $163 for the monthly telephone bill.

Transaction 15   Received the daily cash register summary. Also received deposit slips totaling $3,428.21.

SATURDAY, DECEMBER 6

Transaction 16   Received the daily cash register summary. Also received deposit slips totaling $4,483.32.

SUNDAY, DECEMBER 7

Transaction 17   Received the daily cash register summary. Also received deposit slips totaling $4,515.22.

END-OF-WEEK PROCEDURES

Complete the end-of-week procedures. See page 10.

AUDIT CHECK:

(1) The total of the "Cash Credit" column in the Cash Payments Journal for the week ending December 7 should be $ _13,681.79_

(2) How much does Home Team Advantage owe Duong's Jersey Outlet as of December 7? _$650_

(3) Check Number 614 to Sports Authentica was posted to what account? _A/P_

(4) What were the total credit sales for the week ended December 7? _7,023.56_

(5) The total of the "Cash Debit" column in the Cash Receipts Journal for the week ending December 7 should be $ _24,224.25_

MONDAY, DECEMBER 8

Transaction 18   Issued Check 617 for $2,000 to Texas Racing Association as a security deposit to reserve a merchandise table at the Spring 500 race.

Transaction 19   Issued Check 618 for $12,058.50 to Duong's Jersey Outlet for basketball jerseys for Invoice 608 dated November 29.

Transaction 20   Issued Check 619 for $99 to Sentinel Alarms for monthly service.

Transaction 21   Received the daily cash register summary. Also received deposit slips totaling $2,523.52.

TUESDAY, DECEMBER 9

Transaction 22   Issued Check 620 for $735 to Woodworks, Inc. for baseball bat display cases for Invoice 2932 dated December 1 less 2 percent discount.

Transaction 23   Purchased signed basketballs from Autograph Central for $2,000; terms 2/10, n/30; Invoice 2341 dated December 8.

Transaction 24   Issued Check 621 for $3,136 to International Sports Supplies for a November invoice less the 2 percent discount.

Transaction 25   Issued Check 622 for $9,222.50 to Texas State Department of Revenue for sales tax collected during November.

Transaction 26   Received the daily cash register summary. Also received deposit slips totaling $2,174.12.

WEDNESDAY, DECEMBER 10

Transaction 27   Give credit Memorandum 89 for $40 to Monica Mooney, a charge account customer, for damaged merchandise sold to her on December 3.

Transaction 28   Purchased 20 autographed baseballs for $1,000 from Sports Authentica; terms 30 days net; Invoice 123 dated December 7.

Transaction 29   Issued Check 623 for $253.21 to Office Staples for various supplies.

Transaction 30   Received the daily cash register summary. Also received deposit slips
                  totaling $2,314.35.

THURSDAY, DECEMBER 11

Transaction 31   Purchased autographed die-cast cars from Calderon Sports Supply for
                  $800; terms 5/10, n/30; Invoice 421 dated December 8.

Transaction 32   Purchased die-cast car display units from Woodworks, Inc. for $450; terms
                  2/10, n/30; Invoice 2967 dated December 8.

Transaction 33   Received the daily cash register summary. Also received deposit slips
                  totaling $3,214.21.

FRIDAY, DECEMBER 12

Transaction 34   Issued Check 624 for $45.23 to Office Staples for printer, facsimile, and
                  copy machine paper.

Transaction 35   Issued Check 625 for $78 to U.S. Post Office for 4 rolls of stamps.

Transaction 36   Received the daily cash register summary. Also received deposit slips
                  totaling $3,255.50.

SATURDAY, DECEMBER 13

Transaction 37   Received the daily cash register summary. Also received deposit slips
                  totaling $4,586.36.

SUNDAY, DECEMBER 14

Transaction 38   Received the daily cash register summary. Also received deposit slips
                  totaling $5,255.23.

END-OF-WEEK PROCEDURES

Complete the end-of-week procedures. See page 10.

AUDIT CHECK:

(1) The total of the "Cash Credit" column in the Cash Payments Journal for the period from
     December 1 to December 14 should be $_____.

(2) How much does Home Team Advantage owe Sports Authentica as of December 14?

(3) Check Number 624 to Office Staples was posted to what account?

(4) How much does Jamaal Howard owe Home Team Advantage as of December 14?

(5) The total of the "Cash Debit" column in the Cash Receipts Journal for the period from
     December 1 to December 14 should be $_____.

MONDAY, DECEMBER 15

Transaction 39   Record the semimonthly payroll.

(1) Make a general journal entry to record the total payroll for December 1-15. The payroll
     summary provided by the automated payroll service is shown:

PAYROLL SYSTEMS INC
PAYROLL SUMMARY
COMPANY NAME: HOME TEAM ADVANTAGE, INC.
PAY PERIOD ENDING: DECEMBER 15, 20—

DEPARTMENT NUMBER	DEPARTMENT	DEDUCTIONS				
		GROSS EARNINGS	SOCIAL SECURITY	MEDICARE TAX	FEDERAL INCOME TAX	NET PAY
601	SALES	3,240	201	47	486	2,506
602	OFFICE	4,320	268	62	1,210	2,780
603	STOCKROOM	1,160	72	17	174	897
TOTALS		8,720	541	126	1,870	6,183

(a) The business has separate expense accounts for sales, office, and stockroom salaries. The payroll summary lists the gross earnings by department. Debit the amount for each department to the appropriate expense account.

(b) Credit the total of each deduction to the appropriate liability account.

(c) Credit the total pay to Salaries Payable.

(2) Make a general journal entry to record the employer's social security and Medicare tax liability of $667 (sum of employer's matching share of social security withheld of $541 and Medicare withheld of $126). Debit Payroll Taxes Expense and credit Payroll Taxes Payable in accordance with the established procedure used at Home Team Advantage, Inc. (An alternative accounting procedure is to credit the specific tax liability accounts.)

(3) Issue Check 626 for the total pay to Home Team Advantage Payroll account in order to transfer the   necessary funds from the regular checking account. Enter this check in the cash payments journal, with the amount debited to Salaries Payable in the Other Accounts Debit column.

Transaction 40   Issued Check 627 for $441 to Woodworks, Inc. for die-cast car display units for Invoice 2967 dated December 8 less 2 percent.

Transaction 41   Issued Check 628 for $1,960 to Autograph Central for autographed basketballs for Invoice 2341 dated December 8 less the 2 percent discount.

Transaction 42   Received the daily cash register summary. Also received deposit slips totaling $2,324.92.

TUESDAY, DECEMBER 16

Transaction 43   Issued Check 629 for $2,000 to Lone Star Hockey Club for in-store promotion.

Transaction 44   Purchased case of hockey pucks for $500 from Sports Authentica; terms 30 days net; Invoice 197 dated December 16.

Transaction 45   Issued Check 630 for $760 to Calderon Sports Supply for autographed die-cast cars for Invoice 421 dated December 8 less 5 percent discount.

Home Team Advantage Practice Set

Transaction 46   Received the daily cash register summary. Also received deposit slips totaling $2,572.32.

WEDNESDAY, DECEMBER 17

Transaction 47   Issued Check 631 for $122.32 to Ground Delivery for delivery charges.

Transaction 48   Received Credit Memorandum 234 for $100 from International Sports Supply as an allowance to compensate for shipment of damaged merchandise in November.

Transaction 49   Received the daily cash register summary. Also received deposit slips totaling $3,252.11

THURSDAY, DECEMBER 18

Transaction 50   Issued Check 632 for $349.99 to Dallas Digital Networks for monthly cellular phone service and high-speed Internet access bill.

Transaction 51   Received the daily cash register summary. Also received deposit slips totaling $3,218.56

FRIDAY, DECEMBER 19

Transaction 52   Issued Check 633 for $3,204 to First Bank of Texas for deposit of amounts withheld from employees' earnings for the semimonthly payroll period ended December 15 and employer's share of social security and Medicare tax as follows:

Social Security Tax Withheld	$541.00
Medicare Tax Withheld	126.00
Federal Income Tax Withheld	1,870.00
Social Security Tax – Employer's Share	541.00
Medicare Tax – Employer's Share	126.00

Debit the payment of employer's share of payroll taxes to Payroll Taxes Payable.

Transaction 53   Issued Check 634 for $1,000 to Bracket Sports Collector magazine for advertising purchased in November.

Transaction 54   Received the daily cash register summary. Also received deposit slips totaling $3,429.39.

SATURDAY, DECEMBER 20

Transaction 55   Received the daily cash register summary. Also received deposit slips totaling $4,983.24.

SUNDAY, DECEMBER 21

Transaction 56   Received the daily cash register summary. Also received deposit slips totaling $4,823.09.

END-OF-WEEK PROCEDURES

Complete the end-of-week procedures.

AUDIT CHECK:

(1) The total of the "Cash Credit" column in the Cash Payments Journal for the period from December 1 to December 21 should be $ 60,084.54

(2) What is the balance of the Payroll Taxes Payable account as of December 21?

(3) How much does Jean Kim owe Home Team Advantage, Inc. as of December 21?

(4) What is the balance of the Sports Authentica account as of December 21?

(5) The total of the "Cash Debit" column in the Cash Receipts Journal for the period from December 1 to December 21 should be $72,153.17

MONDAY, DECEMBER 22

Transaction 57   Issued Check 635 for $1,200 to Catalog Master for holiday mailer design and postage.

Transaction 58   Issued Check 636 for $500.00 to Dallas Softball League for sponsorship of team.

Transaction 59   Purchased 30 cases of boxing videotapes from Ringside Entertainment for $600; terms 2/10, n/30; Invoice 6291 dated December 20.

Transaction 60   Received the daily cash register summary. Also received deposit slips totaling $2,034.83.

TUESDAY, DECEMBER 23

Transaction 61   Issued Check 637 for $234 to Ground Delivery for delivery charges.

Transaction 62   Issued Check 638 for $158 to Ron Morris to reimburse gas and meal expenses during trade show.

Transaction 63   Received the daily cash register summary. Also received deposit slips totaling $2,151.58.

WEDNESDAY, DECEMBER 24

Transaction 64   Purchased six boxes of action figures from Toy Warehouse for $2,400; terms 30 days net; Invoice 2532 dated December 22.

Transaction 65   Purchased 100 autographed portraits from Worldwide Tennis for $300; terms 2/10, n/30; Invoice 5213 dated December 23.

Transaction 66   Issued Check 639 for $249.99 to Bell Security for monthly security services.

Transaction 67   Received the daily cash register summary. Also received deposit slips totaling $1,235.52.

THURSDAY, DECEMBER 25

Store closed for holiday.

FRIDAY, DECEMBER 26

Transaction 68   Issued Check 640 for $1,000 to Sports Authentica for autographed baseballs; Invoice 123 dated December 7.

Transaction 69   Issued Check 641 for $512 to Ground Delivery for delivery charges.

Transaction 70   Received the daily cash register summary. Also received deposit slips totaling $7,234.52.

Home Team Advantage Practice Set

SATURDAY, DECEMBER 27

Transaction 71   Received the daily cash register summary. Also received deposit slips totaling $8,342.56.

SUNDAY, DECEMBER 28

Transaction 72   Received the daily cash register summary. Also received deposit slips totaling $7,778.23. NOTE: Since there are only two more business days in this month, defer end-of-week procedures until the close of business on Wednesday, December 31.

MONDAY, DECEMBER 29

Transaction 73   Issued Check 642 for $588 to Ringside Entertainment for 30 cases of boxing videotapes for Invoice 6291 dated December 20 less 2 percent discount.

Transaction 74   Purchased soccer banners and jerseys from International Sports Supplies for $1,200; terms 2/10, n/30; Invoice 6982 dated December 26.

Transaction 75   Received the daily cash register summary. Also received deposit slips totaling $4,231.64.

TUESDAY, DECEMBER 30

Transaction 76   Issued Check 643 for $500 to Sports Authentica for a case of hockey pucks for Invoice 197 dated December 16.

Transaction 77   Gave Credit Memorandum 622 for $231.41 to Wendy Gau for a return of merchandise sold to her on December 19.

Transaction 78   Received the daily cash register summary. Also received deposit slips totaling $8,936.35

WEDNESDAY, DECEMBER 31

Transaction 79   Received the daily cash register summary. Also received deposit slips totaling $1,541.23.

Transaction 80   Issued Check 644 for $4,000 to Dan Morris as his withdrawal for the month.

Transaction 81   Record $259.66 as bank credit card discount in the Cash Payments Journal.

Transaction 82   Record the semimonthly payroll.

(1) Make a general journal entry to record the total payroll for December 16-31. The payroll summary provided by the automated payroll service is shown:

PAYROLL SYSTEMS INC
PAYROLL SUMMARY
COMPANY NAME: HOME TEAM ADVANTAGE, INC.
PAY PERIOD ENDING: DECEMBER 15, 20—

DEPARTMENT NUMBER	DEPARTMENT	DEDUCTIONS				
		GROSS EARNINGS	SOCIAL SECURITY	MEDICARE TAX	FEDERAL INCOME TAX	NET PAY
601	SALES	3,240	201	47	486	2,506
602	OFFICE	4,320	268	62	1,210	2,780
603	STOCKROOM	1,160	72	17	174	897
TOTALS		8,720	541	126	1,870	6,183

(a) The business has separate expense accounts for sales, office, and stockroom salaries. The payroll summary lists the gross earnings by department. Debit the amount for each department to the appropriate expense account.

(b) Credit the total of each deduction to the appropriate liability account.

(c) Credit the total pay to Salaries Payable.

(2) Make a general journal entry to record the employer's social security and Medicare tax liability of $667 (sum of employer's matching share of social security withheld of $541 and Medicare withheld of $126). Debit Payroll Taxes Expense and credit Payroll Taxes Payable in accordance with the established procedure used at Home Team Advantage, Inc. (An alternative accounting procedure is to credit the specific tax liability accounts.)

(3) Issue Check 645 for the total pay to Home Team Advantage Payroll account in order to transfer the necessary funds from the regular checking account. Enter this check in the cash payments journal, with the amount debited to Salaries Payable in the Other Accounts Debit column.

END-OF-WEEK PROCEDURES
Complete the following end-of-week procedures.

AUDIT CHECK:
(1) The total of the "Cash Credit" column in the Cash Payments Journal for the period from December 1 to December 31 should be $_____.

(2) How much does Home Team Advantage, Inc. owe Toy Warehouse as of December 31?

(3) Check 639 to Bell Security was posted to what account?

(4) How much does Linda Padilla owe Home Team Advantage as of December 31?

(5) The total of the "Cash Debit" column in the Cash Receipts Journal for the period from December 1 to December 31 should be $_____.

MONTHLY PROCEDURES

END-OF-MONTH PROCEDURES

All regular transactions for the month of December have now been recorded. Complete the following end-of-month procedures.

(1) Since the footings have been entered and proved in each special journal, total and rule these journals.

(2) Verify that all individual postings to the general ledger have been made from the general journal and the Other Accounts columns of the cash receipts and cash payments journals.

(3) Make the required summary postings of the column totals from the special journals (except the totals of the Other Accounts columns) to the proper general ledger accounts.

(4) Prepare a schedule of accounts receivable as of December 31, 20--, and prove the total by comparing it with the balance of the Accounts Receivable accounts ($19,171.98). If the two amounts do not agree, check your work before proceeding.

(5) Prepare a schedule of accounts payable as of December 31, 20--, and prove the total by comparing it with the balance of the Accounts Payable account ($3,800.00). If the two amounts do not agree, check your work before proceeding.

(6) Prepare a trial balance to prove the accuracy of the general ledger accounts as of December 31, 20--. Use the ten-column worksheet. This will enable you to save time in completing the end-of-year procedures. List the names of all general ledger accounts, including Income Summary 399, whether or not the accounts have balances. Verify the equality of the debit and credit totals. If these totals are not equal ($1,364,224.96), check your work before proceeding.

END-OF-YEAR PROCEDURES

The fiscal year of Home Team Advantage ends on December 31. You are now ready to perform the necessary end-of-year procedures.

(1) Record the following adjustments on the worksheet.

    (a-b) Enter the adjustment for merchandise inventory on the worksheet. The ending inventory is $172,482.11. Use the letters *a* and *b* for these adjustments.

    (c) Uncollectible accounts expense is estimated at one-half of 1 percent of net credit sales. An analysis of the year's sales shows net credit sales to be $206,928. Make an adjustment for the estimated uncollectible accounts. Use the letter *c* to identify this adjustment.

    (d) On October 1, 20--, Home Team Advantage purchased a one-year, $35,000 U.S. Treasury note that has an interest rate of 4.5 percent. The firm will receive the interest in cash at the end of each six-month period. Therefore it is necessary to accrue the interest earned in October, November, and December 20--. Use the letter *d* to identify this adjustment. (Use the formula Principal x Rate x Time to compute the accrued interest.)

    (e) Analysis of the firm's insurance policies shows that $2,798 of the premiums currently recorded in the Prepaid Insurance account represents coverage that has expired. Record an adjustment for the expired amount. Use the letter e to identify this adjustment.

(f) A physical inventory of the store supplies show items totaling $260 on hand as of December 31. Make an adjustment for the store supplies used during the fiscal year. Identify this adjustment with the letter f.

(g) A physical inventory of the office supplies show items totaling $498 on hand as of December 31. Make an adjustment for the office supplies used during the fiscal year. Identify this adjustment with the letter g.

(h) The firm's depreciation schedule shows that $6,570 in depreciation should be taken for the fiscal year ended December 31, 20--. Use the letter h to identify the adjustment for depreciation.

(i) The firm owes $2,348 of federal and state unemployment taxes for the quarter ended December 31. Credit Payroll Taxes Payable for the amount. Use the letter i to identify the adjustment. (It is not necessary to accrue the employer's share of the social security and Medicare tax, since the liability for these taxes was recorded as part of the semimonthly payroll entries.)

(2) Foot the figures in the Adjustment columns of the worksheet, verify the equality of the debit and credit totals, and then enter the totals and rule the columns.

(3) Complete the Adjusted Trial Balance section. Combine the trial balance figures and the adjustments and extend the resulting amounts into the Adjusted Trial Balance columns. Foot and prove these columns, verify the equality of the debit and credit totals, enter the totals, and rule the columns.

(4) Complete the Income Statement and Balance Sheet sections.

(a) Extend the balances of the asset, liability, and owner's equity accounts to the Balance Sheet columns.

(b) Extend the balances of the revenue, cost and expense accounts to the income statement columns.

(c) Foot the figures in the four columns, determine the net income and transfer it from the Income Statement section to the Balance Sheet section. The net income should be $65,966.09.

(d) Enter the subtotals, bring down the final totals in all columns, verify the equality of the debit and credit totals, and rule the columns.

(5) Prepare an income statement for the fiscal year ended December 31, 20--. The income statement from the previous fiscal year is illustrated on page 21. Use it as a guide. The $65,966.09 net income for the year computed on the worksheet must agree with the net income for the period as shown on the income statement.

FIGURE 6

HOME TEAM ADVANTAGE
INCOME STATEMENT
YEAR ENDED DECEMBER 31, 2005

OPERATING REVENUE			
Sales		$ 955,018.25	
Less Sales Returns and Allowances		17,880.20	
Net Sales			$ 937,138.05
COST OF GOODS SOLD			
Merchandise Inventory, January 1, 2005		198,732.35	
Merchandise Purchases	$ 488,072.17		
Freight In	18,106.75		
Delivered Cost of Purchases	506,178.92		
Less Purchases Returns and Allowances	$ 7,900.50		
Purchase Discounts	6,473.41	14,373.91	
Net Delivered Cost of Purchases		491,805.01	
Total Merchandise Available for Sale		690,537.36	
Less Merchandise Inventory, December 31, 2005		198,221.75	
Cost of Goods Sold			492,315.61
Gross Profit			444,822.44
OPERATING EXPENSES			
Sales Salaries Expense		77,760.00	
Office Salaries Expense		103,680.00	
Stockroom Salaries Expense		27,840.00	
Payroll Taxes Expense		16,008.00	
Rent Expense		28,800.00	
Utilities Expense		5,917.32	
Telecommunications Expense		6,872.26	
Store Supplies		528.92	
Office Supplies		1,946.82	
Security Expense		1,188.00	
Advertising Expense		21,000.00	
Rubbish Removal Expense		3,600.00	
Uncollectible Accounts Expense		4,063.00	
Trade Show Expense		2,700.00	
Credit Card Discount Expense		2,557.79	
Depreciation Expense		6,552.00	
Total Operating Expenses			311,014.11
Income from Operations			133,808.33
OTHER INCOME			
Interest Income		2,000.00	
OTHER EXPENSE			
Interest Expense		4,000.00	
Net Nonoperating Expense			2,000.00
Net Income			$ 131,808.33

FIGURE 7

HOME TEAM ADVANTAGE
STATEMENT OF OWNER'S EQUITY
YEAR ENDED DECEMBER 31, 2005

Dan Morris, Capital, January 1, 2005		$ 217,517.05
Net Income For Year	$ 131,808.33	
Less Withdrawals for the Year	48,000.00	
Increase in Capital		83,808.33
Dan Morris, Capital, December 31, 2005		$ 301,325.38

FIGURE 8

HOME TEAM ADVANTAGE
BALANCE SHEET
December 31, 2005

ASSETS
CURRENT ASSETS

Cash		$ 69,662.65	
Petty Cash Fund		50.00	
Short-Term Investments		5,000.00	
Accounts Receivable	$ 20,068.00		
Less Allowance for Uncollectible Accounts	515.43	19,552.57	
Interest Receivable		150.00	
Security Deposits		350.00	
Merchandise Inventory		198,221.75	
Prepaid Expenses:			
Prepaid Insurance	937.50		
Store Supplies	1,079.00		
Office Supplies	298.00	2,314.50	
Total Current Assets			$ 295,301.47
EQUIPMENT			
Store Fixtures and Equipment		36,400.00	
Less Accumulated Depreciation		6,552.00	
Total Equipment			29,848.00
TOTAL ASSETS			$ 325,149.47

LIABILITIES AND OWNER'S EQUITY
CURRENT LIABILITIES

Accounts Payable		$ 14,372.50	
Social Security Tax Payable		541.00	
Medicare Tax Payable		126.00	
Federal Income Tax Payable		1,870.00	
Payroll Taxes Payable		667.00	
Sales Tax Payable		6,247.59	
Total Current Liabilities			$ 23,824.09
OWNER'S EQUITY			
Dan Morris, Capital			301,325.38
TOTAL LIABILITIES AND OWNER'S EQUITY			$ 325,149.47

Home Team Advantage Practice Set

ADUSTING AND CLOSING PROCEDURES

You are now ready to complete the adjusting and closing procedures.

(1)   In the general journal, record the adjusting entries for the accounting period.

(2)   Post the adjusting entries to the general ledger.

(3)   In the general journal, close the revenue and other temporary accounts with credit balances except the Income Summary account.

(4)   In the general journal, close all the expense accounts and other temporary accounts with debit balances except the Income Summary account.

(5)   Post the first two closing entries to the general ledger.

(6)   In the general journal, record the entry to transfer the net income to the owner's capital accounts.

(7)   In the general journal, record the entry to close the owner's drawing account.

(8)   Post the last two closing entries to the general ledger.

(9)   Prepare a postclosing trial balance as of December 31, 20--. Make sure that the debit and credit totals are equal.

(10)   In the general journal, record any reversing entries that may be necessary. Date these entries January 1, 20--.

(11)   Post the reversing entries to the general ledger.

NOTE: Your instructor will indicate which materials you are to submit.

Cash Register
Summaries

Home Team Advantage Practice Set

CASH REGISTER SUMMARY

CASH COLLECTIONS   12/01/20--

CUSTOMER NO.	SOURCE	ACCTS. REC. COLLECTED	AMOUNT OF SALE	SALES TAX	CASH RECEIVED
	Cash Sales		577.51	46.20	623.71
	Bank Credit Card Sales		1,186.34	94.91	1,281.25
2369	Steve Carlyle	72.15			72.15
	TOTALS	72.15	1,763.85	141.11	1,977.11

CHARGE ACCOUNT SALES

CUSTOMER NO.	CUSTOMER NAME		AMOUNT OF SALE	SALES TAX	TOTAL RECEIVABLE
2984	Jamaal Howard		118.06	9.44	127.50
	TOTALS		118.06	9.44	127.50

CASH REGISTER SUMMARY

CASH COLLECTIONS   12/02/20--

CUSTOMER NO.	SOURCE	ACCTS. REC. COLLECTED	AMOUNT OF SALE	SALES TAX	CASH RECEIVED
	Cash Sales		1,435.74	114.86	1,550.60
	Bank Credit Card Sales		307.12	24.57	331.69
1089	Rick Marquez	1,547.06			1,547.06
	TOTALS	1,547.06	1,742.86	139.43	3,429.35

CHARGE ACCOUNT SALES

CUSTOMER NO.	CUSTOMER NAME		AMOUNT OF SALE	SALES TAX	TOTAL RECEIVABLE
6281	Gia Marakas		925.00	74.00	999.00
	TOTALS		925.00	74.00	999.00

CASH REGISTER SUMMARY

CASH COLLECTIONS

12/03/20--

CUSTOMER NO.	SOURCE	ACCTS. REC. COLLECTED	AMOUNT OF SALE	SALES TAX	CASH RECEIVED
	Cash Sales		1,275.18	102.01	1,377.19
	Bank Credit Card Sales		1,443.62	115.49	1,559.11
2745	Michelle Weinstein	487.22			487.22
	TOTALS	487.22	2,718.80	217.50	3,423.52

CHARGE ACCOUNT SALES

CUSTOMER NO.	CUSTOMER NAME		AMOUNT OF SALE	SALES TAX	TOTAL RECEIVABLE
6770	Marques Miller		880.50	70.44	950.94
	TOTALS		880.50	70.44	950.94

CASH REGISTER SUMMARY

CASH COLLECTIONS

12/04/20--

CUSTOMER NO.	SOURCE	ACCTS. REC. COLLECTED	AMOUNT OF SALE	SALES TAX	CASH RECEIVED
	Cash Sales		1,147.23	91.78	1,239.01
	Bank Credit Card Sales		213.44	17.07	230.51
4316	Laurie Chapman	1,500.00			1,500.00
	TOTALS	1,500.00	1,360.67	108.85	2,969.52

CHARGE ACCOUNT SALES

CUSTOMER NO.	CUSTOMER NAME		AMOUNT OF SALE	SALES TAX	TOTAL RECEIVABLE
	TOTALS				

Home Team Advantage Practice Set

CASH REGISTER SUMMARY

CASH COLLECTIONS

12/05/20--

CUSTOMER NO.	SOURCE	ACCTS. REC. COLLECTED	AMOUNT OF SALE	SALES TAX	CASH RECEIVED
	Cash Sales		3,174.27	253.94	3,428.21
	Bank Credit Card Sales				
	TOTALS		3,174.27	253.94	3,428.21

CHARGE ACCOUNT SALES

CUSTOMER NO.	CUSTOMER NAME	AMOUNT OF SALE	SALES TAX	TOTAL RECEIVABLE
9623	Jeff Briggs	70.83	5.67	76.50
9672	Monica Mooney	423.04	33.84	456.88
	TOTALS	493.87	39.51	533.38

CASH REGISTER SUMMARY

CASH COLLECTIONS

12/06/20--

CUSTOMER NO.	SOURCE	ACCTS. REC. COLLECTED	AMOUNT OF SALE	SALES TAX	CASH RECEIVED
	Cash Sales		1,055.09	84.41	1,139.50
	Bank Credit Card Sales		3,096.13	247.69	3,343.82
	TOTALS		4,151.22	332.10	4,483.32

CHARGE ACCOUNT SALES

CUSTOMER NO.	CUSTOMER NAME	AMOUNT OF SALE	SALES TAX	TOTAL RECEIVABLE
	TOTALS			

CASH REGISTER SUMMARY

CASH COLLECTIONS

12/07/20--

CUSTOMER NO.	SOURCE	ACCTS. REC. COLLECTED	AMOUNT OF SALE	SALES TAX	CASH RECEIVED
	Cash Sales		3,792.24	303.38	4,095.62
	Bank Credit Card Sales				
3118	Dave Jordan	137.47			137.47
4277	Kristen Boucher	282.13			282.13
	TOTALS	419.60	3,792.24	303.38	4,515.22

CHARGE ACCOUNT SALES

CUSTOMER NO.	CUSTOMER NAME	AMOUNT OF SALE	SALES TAX	TOTAL RECEIVABLE
1089	Rick Marquez	405.32	32.43	437.75
2369	Steve Carlyle	4,200.81	336.07	4,536.88
	TOTALS	4,606.13	368.50	4,974.63

CASH REGISTER SUMMARY

CASH COLLECTIONS

12/08/20--

CUSTOMER NO.	SOURCE	ACCTS. REC. COLLECTED	AMOUNT OF SALE	SALES TAX	CASH RECEIVED
	Cash Sales		1,506.19	120.50	1,626.69
	Bank Credit Card Sales		367.13	29.37	396.50
5081	Brad Smythe	500.33			500.33
	TOTALS	500.33	1,873.32	149.87	2,523.52

CHARGE ACCOUNT SALES

CUSTOMER NO.	CUSTOMER NAME	AMOUNT OF SALE	SALES TAX	TOTAL RECEIVABLE
5748	Terri Alenikov	54.11	4.33	58.44
	TOTALS	54.11	4.33	58.44

Home Team Advantage Practice Set

CASH REGISTER SUMMARY

CASH COLLECTIONS

12/09/20--

CUSTOMER NO.	SOURCE	ACCTS. REC. COLLECTED	AMOUNT OF SALE	SALES TAX	CASH RECEIVED
	Cash Sales		942.82	75.43	1,018.25
	Bank Credit Card Sales		1,070.25	85.62	1,155.87
	TOTALS		2,013.07	161.05	2,174.12

CHARGE ACCOUNT SALES

CUSTOMER NO.	CUSTOMER NAME		AMOUNT OF SALE	SALES TAX	TOTAL RECEIVABLE
	TOTALS				

CASH REGISTER SUMMARY

CASH COLLECTIONS

12/10/20--

CUSTOMER NO.	SOURCE	ACCTS. REC. COLLECTED	AMOUNT OF SALE	SALES TAX	CASH RECEIVED
	Cash Sales		1,207.12	96.57	1,303.69
	Bank Credit Card Sales		267.74	21.42	289.16
6443	Wendy Gau	721.50			721.50
	TOTALS	721.50	1,474.86	117.99	2,314.35

CHARGE ACCOUNT SALES

CUSTOMER NO.	CUSTOMER NAME		AMOUNT OF SALE	SALES TAX	TOTAL RECEIVABLE
	TOTALS				

CASH REGISTER SUMMARY

CASH COLLECTIONS
12/11/20--

CUSTOMER NO.	SOURCE	ACCTS. REC. COLLECTED	AMOUNT OF SALE	SALES TAX	CASH RECEIVED
	Cash Sales		2,096.49	167.72	2,264.21
	Bank Credit Card Sales				
2369	Steve Carlyle	950.00			950.00
	TOTALS	950.00	2,096.49	167.72	3,214.21

CHARGE ACCOUNT SALES

CUSTOMER NO.	CUSTOMER NAME	AMOUNT OF SALE	SALES TAX	TOTAL RECEIVABLE
2745	Michelle Weinstein	1,229.75	98.38	1,328.13
	TOTALS	1,229.75	98.38	1,328.13

CASH REGISTER SUMMARY

CASH COLLECTIONS
12/12/20--

CUSTOMER NO.	SOURCE	ACCTS. REC. COLLECTED	AMOUNT OF SALE	SALES TAX	CASH RECEIVED
	Cash Sales		2,862.01	228.96	3,090.97
	Bank Credit Card Sales		152.34	12.19	164.53
	TOTALS		3,014.35	241.15	3,255.50

CHARGE ACCOUNT SALES

CUSTOMER NO.	CUSTOMER NAME	AMOUNT OF SALE	SALES TAX	TOTAL RECEIVABLE
	TOTALS			

CASH REGISTER SUMMARY

CASH COLLECTIONS

12/13/20--

CUSTOMER NO.	SOURCE	ACCTS. REC. COLLECTED	AMOUNT OF SALE	SALES TAX	CASH RECEIVED
	Cash Sales		3,754.18	300.33	4,054.51
	Bank Credit Card Sales		492.45	39.40	531.85
	TOTALS		4,246.63	339.73	4,586.36

CHARGE ACCOUNT SALES

CUSTOMER NO.	CUSTOMER NAME		AMOUNT OF SALE	SALES TAX	TOTAL RECEIVABLE
6907	Ann Roff		609.95	48.80	658.75
	TOTALS		609.95	48.80	658.75

CASH REGISTER SUMMARY

CASH COLLECTIONS

12/14/20--

CUSTOMER NO.	SOURCE	ACCTS. REC. COLLECTED	AMOUNT OF SALE	SALES TAX	CASH RECEIVED
	Cash Sales		1,881.02	150.48	2,031.50
	Bank Credit Card Sales		2,334.12	186.73	2,520.85
6907	Ann Roff	702.88			702.88
	TOTALS	702.88	4,215.14	337.21	5,255.23

CHARGE ACCOUNT SALES

CUSTOMER NO.	CUSTOMER NAME		AMOUNT OF SALE	SALES TAX	TOTAL RECEIVABLE
3118	Dave Jordan		1,844.62	147.57	1,992.19
	TOTALS		1,844.62	147.57	1,992.19

CASH REGISTER SUMMARY

CASH COLLECTIONS   12/15/20--

CUSTOMER NO.	SOURCE	ACCTS. REC. COLLECTED	AMOUNT OF SALE	SALES TAX	CASH RECEIVED
	Cash Sales		504.61	40.37	544.98
	Bank Credit Card Sales		1,558.17	124.65	1,682.82
7651	Mike Antonello	97.12			97.12
	TOTALS	97.12	2,062.78	165.02	2,324.92

CHARGE ACCOUNT SALES

CUSTOMER NO.	CUSTOMER NAME		AMOUNT OF SALE	SALES TAX	TOTAL RECEIVABLE
4277	Kristen Boucher		615.82	49.27	665.09
	TOTALS		615.82	49.27	665.09

CASH REGISTER SUMMARY

CASH COLLECTIONS   12/16/20--

CUSTOMER NO.	SOURCE	ACCTS. REC. COLLECTED	AMOUNT OF SALE	SALES TAX	CASH RECEIVED
	Cash Sales		519.27	41.54	560.81
	Bank Credit Card Sales		1,862.51	149.00	2,011.51
	TOTALS		2,381.78	190.54	2,572.32

CHARGE ACCOUNT SALES

CUSTOMER NO.	CUSTOMER NAME		AMOUNT OF SALE	SALES TAX	TOTAL RECEIVABLE
	TOTALS				

CASH REGISTER SUMMARY

CASH COLLECTIONS   12/17/20--

CUSTOMER NO.	SOURCE	ACCTS. REC. COLLECTED	AMOUNT OF SALE	SALES TAX	CASH RECEIVED
	Cash Sales		2,853.19	228.25	3,081.44
	Bank Credit Card Sales		88.47	7.08	95.55
5748	Terry Alenikov	75.12			75.12
	TOTALS	75.12	2,941.66	235.33	3,252.11

CHARGE ACCOUNT SALES

CUSTOMER NO.	CUSTOMER NAME	AMOUNT OF SALE	SALES TAX	TOTAL RECEIVABLE
5081	Brad Smythe	2,149.59	171.97	2,321.56
	TOTALS	2,149.59	171.97	2,321.56

CASH REGISTER SUMMARY

CASH COLLECTIONS   12/18/20--

CUSTOMER NO.	SOURCE	ACCTS. REC. COLLECTED	AMOUNT OF SALE	SALES TAX	CASH RECEIVED
	Cash Sales		2,980.15	238.41	3,218.56
	Bank Credit Card Sales				
	TOTALS		2,980.15	238.41	3,218.56

CHARGE ACCOUNT SALES

CUSTOMER NO.	CUSTOMER NAME	AMOUNT OF SALE	SALES TAX	TOTAL RECEIVABLE
7805	Kathy Oh	177.17	14.17	191.34
	TOTALS	177.17	14.17	191.34

CASH REGISTER SUMMARY

CASH COLLECTIONS   12/19/20--

CUSTOMER NO.	SOURCE	ACCTS. REC. COLLECTED	AMOUNT OF SALE	SALES TAX	CASH RECEIVED
	Cash Sales		2,263.20	181.06	2,444.26
	Bank Credit Card Sales		912.16	72.97	985.13
	TOTALS		3,175.36	254.03	3,429.39

CHARGE ACCOUNT SALES

CUSTOMER NO.	CUSTOMER NAME		AMOUNT OF SALE	SALES TAX	TOTAL RECEIVABLE
6443	Wendy Gau		713.25	57.06	770.31
	TOTALS		713.25	57.06	770.31

CASH REGISTER SUMMARY

CASH COLLECTIONS   12/20/20--

CUSTOMER NO.	SOURCE	ACCTS. REC. COLLECTED	AMOUNT OF SALE	SALES TAX	CASH RECEIVED
	Cash Sales		2,630.08	210.41	2,840.49
	Bank Credit Card Sales		1,984.03	158.72	2,142.75
	TOTALS		4,614.11	369.13	4,983.24

CHARGE ACCOUNT SALES

CUSTOMER NO.	CUSTOMER NAME		AMOUNT OF SALE	SALES TAX	TOTAL RECEIVABLE
7651	Mike Antonello		322.19	25.78	347.97
	TOTALS		322.19	25.78	347.97

Home Team Advantage Practice Set

CASH REGISTER SUMMARY

CASH COLLECTIONS   12/21/20--

CUSTOMER NO.	SOURCE	ACCTS. REC. COLLECTED	AMOUNT OF SALE	SALES TAX	CASH RECEIVED
	Cash Sales		838.68	67.10	905.78
	Bank Credit Card Sales		3,627.14	290.17	3,917.31
	TOTALS		4,465.82	357.27	4,823.09

CHARGE ACCOUNT SALES

CUSTOMER NO.	CUSTOMER NAME		AMOUNT OF SALE	SALES TAX	TOTAL RECEIVABLE
	TOTALS				

CASH REGISTER SUMMARY

CASH COLLECTIONS   12/22/20--

CUSTOMER NO.	SOURCE	ACCTS. REC. COLLECTED	AMOUNT OF SALE	SALES TAX	CASH RECEIVED
	Cash Sales		706.49	56.52	763.01
	Bank Credit Card Sales		1,020.94	81.67	1,102.61
7805	Kathy Oh	169.21			169.21
	TOTALS	169.21	1,727.43	138.19	2,034.83

CHARGE ACCOUNT SALES

CUSTOMER NO.	CUSTOMER NAME		AMOUNT OF SALE	SALES TAX	TOTAL RECEIVABLE
7649	Linda Padilla		509.61	40.77	550.38
	TOTALS		509.61	40.77	550.38

CASH REGISTER SUMMARY

CASH COLLECTIONS

12/23/20--

CUSTOMER NO.	SOURCE	ACCTS. REC. COLLECTED	AMOUNT OF SALE	SALES TAX	CASH RECEIVED
	Cash Sales		1,492.90	119.43	1,612.33
	Bank Credit Card Sales		499.30	39.95	539.25
	TOTALS		1,992.20	159.38	2,151.58

CHARGE ACCOUNT SALES

CUSTOMER NO.	CUSTOMER NAME	AMOUNT OF SALE	SALES TAX	TOTAL RECEIVABLE
4316	Laurie Chapman	723.25	57.83	781.11 08
	TOTALS	723.25	57.83	781.11 08

CASH REGISTER SUMMARY

CASH COLLECTIONS

12/24/20--

CUSTOMER NO.	SOURCE	ACCTS. REC. COLLECTED	AMOUNT OF SALE	SALES TAX	CASH RECEIVED
	Cash Sales		56.88	4.55	61.43
	Bank Credit Card Sales		1,038.27	83.06	1,121.33
9672	Monica Mooney	52.76			52.76
	TOTALS	52.76	1,095.15	87.61	1,235.52

CHARGE ACCOUNT SALES

CUSTOMER NO.	CUSTOMER NAME	AMOUNT OF SALE	SALES TAX	TOTAL RECEIVABLE
	TOTALS			

CASH REGISTER SUMMARY

CASH COLLECTIONS   **12/26/20--**

CUSTOMER NO.	SOURCE	ACCTS. REC. COLLECTED	AMOUNT OF SALE	SALES TAX	CASH RECEIVED
	Cash Sales		2,136.32	170.91	2,307.23
	Bank Credit Card Sales		4,146.99	331.76	4,478.75
9864	Debbie Gutierrez	448.54			448.54
	TOTALS	448.54	6,283.31	502.67	7,234.52

CHARGE ACCOUNT SALES

CUSTOMER NO.	CUSTOMER NAME	AMOUNT OF SALE	SALES TAX	TOTAL RECEIVABLE
9864	Debbie Gutierrez	626.52	50.12	676.64
	TOTALS	626.52	50.12	676.64

CASH REGISTER SUMMARY

CASH COLLECTIONS   **12/27/20--**

CUSTOMER NO.	SOURCE	ACCTS. REC. COLLECTED	AMOUNT OF SALE	SALES TAX	CASH RECEIVED
	Cash Sales		4,213.72	337.10	4,550.82
	Bank Credit Card Sales		3,392.81	271.43	3,664.24
2984	Jamaal Howard	127.50			127.50
	TOTALS	127.50	7,606.53	608.53	8,342.56

CHARGE ACCOUNT SALES

CUSTOMER NO.	CUSTOMER NAME	AMOUNT OF SALE	SALES TAX	TOTAL RECEIVABLE
	TOTALS			

Home Team Advantage Practice Set

CASH REGISTER SUMMARY

CASH COLLECTIONS   **12/28/20--**

CUSTOMER NO.	SOURCE	ACCTS. REC. COLLECTED	AMOUNT OF SALE	SALES TAX	CASH RECEIVED
	Cash Sales		5,199.52	415.96	5,615.48
	Bank Credit Card Sales		2,002.55	160.20	2,162.75
	TOTALS		7,202.07	576.16	7,778.23

CHARGE ACCOUNT SALES

CUSTOMER NO.	CUSTOMER NAME		AMOUNT OF SALE	SALES TAX	TOTAL RECEIVABLE
	TOTALS				

CASH REGISTER SUMMARY

CASH COLLECTIONS   **12/29/20--**

CUSTOMER NO.	SOURCE	ACCTS. REC. COLLECTED	AMOUNT OF SALE	SALES TAX	CASH RECEIVED
	Cash Sales		2,112.69	169.01	2,281.70
	Bank Credit Card Sales				
6281	Gia Marakas	999.00			999.00
6770	Marques Miller	950.94			950.94
	TOTALS	1,949.94	2,112.69	169.01	4,231.64

CHARGE ACCOUNT SALES

CUSTOMER NO.	CUSTOMER NAME		AMOUNT OF SALE	SALES TAX	TOTAL RECEIVABLE
	TOTALS				

CASH REGISTER SUMMARY

CASH COLLECTIONS   12/30/20--

CUSTOMER NO.	SOURCE	ACCTS. REC. COLLECTED	AMOUNT OF SALE	SALES TAX	CASH RECEIVED
	Cash Sales		1,896.78	151.74	2,048.52
	Bank Credit Card Sales		3,418.83	273.51	3,692.34
6846	Jean Kim	3,195.49			3,195.49
	TOTALS	3,195.49	5,315.61	425.25	8,936.35

CHARGE ACCOUNT SALES

CUSTOMER NO.	CUSTOMER NAME		AMOUNT OF SALE	SALES TAX	TOTAL RECEIVABLE
	TOTALS				

CASH REGISTER SUMMARY

CASH COLLECTIONS   12/31/20--

CUSTOMER NO.	SOURCE	ACCTS. REC. COLLECTED	AMOUNT OF SALE	SALES TAX	CASH RECEIVED
	Cash Sales		1,427.06	114.17	1,541.23
	Bank Credit Card Sales				
	TOTALS		1,427.06	114.17	1,541.23

CHARGE ACCOUNT SALES

CUSTOMER NO.	CUSTOMER NAME		AMOUNT OF SALE	SALES TAX	TOTAL RECEIVABLE
	TOTALS				

Journals

Home Team Advantage Practice Set

SALES JOURNAL

PAGE 35

	DATE	SALES SLIP NO.	CUSTOMER'S ACCOUNT DEBITED	POST REF.	ACCOUNTS RECEIVABLE DEBIT	SALES TAX PAYABLE CREDIT	SALES CREDIT	
1	2013							1
2	Dec 1		Jamal Howard	✓	127 50	9 44	118 06	2
3		2	Gia Marakas	✓	999 00	74 00	925 00	3
4		3	Marques Miller	✓	950 94	70 44	880 50	4
5		5	Jeff Briggs	✓	76 50	5 67	70 83	5
6		5	Monica Mooney	✓	456 88	33 84	423 04	6
7		7	Rick Marquez	✓	437 25	32 43	405 32	7
8		7	Steve Carlyle	✓	4536 88	336 07	4200 81	8
9					7585 45	561 89	7023 56	9
10		8	Terri Alenikov	J38	58 44	4 33	54 11	10
11		11	Michelle Weinstein	J40	1328 13	98 38	1229 75	11
12		13	Ann Roff	J40	658 75	48 80	609 95	12
13		14	Dave Jordan	J40	1992 19	147 57	1844 62	13
14		15	~~Kristen Boucher~~		11622 96	860 97	10761 99	14
15		15	Kristen Boucher	J41	665 09	49 27	615 82	15
16		18	Kathy Oh	J42	191 34	14 17	177 17	16
17		17	Brad Smythe	J42	2321 56	171 97	2149 59	17
18		19	Wendy Gau	J42	770 31	57 06	713 25	18
19		20	Mike Antonello	J42	347 97	25 78	322 19	19
20					15919 23	1179 22	14740 01	20
21		22	Linda Padilla	J44	550 38	40 77	509 61	21
22		23	Laurie Chapman	J44	781 08	57 83	723 25	22
23		26	Debbie Gutierrez	J45	676 64	50 12	626 52	23
24					17927 33	1327 94	16599 39	24
25					17927 33	1327 94	16599 39	25
26					✓ (1141)	✓ (231)	✓ (401)	26
27								27
28								28
29								29
30								30
31								31
32								32
33								33
34								34
35								35
36								36
37								37
38								38

Home Team Advantage Practice Set

Name_____ Date_____ Class_____

CASH RECEIPTS JOURNAL

PAGE 35

#	DATE	EXPLANATION	POST REF	ACCOUNT RECEIVABLE CREDIT	SALES TAX PAYABLE CREDIT	SALES CREDIT	OTHER ACCOUNTS CREDIT — ACCT. TITLE	POST REF	AMOUNT	CASH DEBIT
	2013									
1	Dec 1	Cash Sales	J35		4620	57751				62371
2	1	Bank Credit Card	J35		9491	118634				128125
3	1	Steve Carlyle	J35	7215						7215
4	2	Cash Sales	J35		11486	143574				155060
5	2	Bank Credit Sales	J35		2457	30712				33169
6	2	Rick Marquez	J35	154706						154706
7	3	Cash Sales	J35		10201	127518				137719
8	3	Bank Card Sales	J35		11549	144362				155911
9	3	Michelle Weinstein	J35	48722						48722
10	4	Cash Sales	J35		9178	114723				123901
11	4	Bank Credit Sales	J35		1707	21344				23051
12	4	L. Chapman	J35	150000						150000
13	5	Cash Sales	J35		25394	317427				342821
14	6	Cash Sales	J35		8941	105509				113950
15	6	Bank Credit Sales	J35		24769	309613				334382
16	7	Cash Sales	J35		30338	379224				409562
17	7	D. Jordan	J35	13747						13747
18	7	K. Boucher	J35	28213						28213
19				402663	149631	1870391				2422685
20	8	Cash Sales	J38		12050	150619				162669
21	8	Bank Credit Sales	J38		2937	36713				39650
22	8	Brad Smythe	J38	50033						50033
23	9	Cash Sales	J38		7543	94282				101825
24	9	Bank Credit Sales	J38		8562	107025				115587
25	10	Cash Sales	J39		9657	120712				130369
26	10	Bank Credit Sales	J39		2142	26774				28916
27	10	Wendy Gau	J39	72150						72150
28	11	Cash Sales	J39		16772	209649				226421
29	11	Steve Carlyle	J39	95000						95000
30	12	Cash Sales	J40		22896	286201				309097
31	12	Bank Credit Sales	J40		1219	15234				16453
32	13	Cash Sales	J40		30033	375418				405451
33	13	Bank Credit Sales	J40		3940	49245				53185
34	14	Cash Sales	J40		15048	188102				203150
35	14	Bank Credit Sales	J40		18673	233412				252085
36	14	Ann Roff	J40	70288						70288
37				690074	301103	3763777				4759954

Home Team Advantage Practice Set   Copyright © 2007 The McGraw-Hill Companies

CASH RECEIPTS JOURNAL

PAGE __36__

	DATE	EXPLANATION	POST REF	ACCOUNT RECEIVABLE CREDIT	SALES TAX PAYABLE CREDIT	SALES CREDIT	OTHER ACCOUNTS CREDIT ACCT. TITLE	POST REF	AMOUNT	CASH DEBIT
	Dec 15	Cash Sales	J41		40 37	504 61				544 98
1	15	Bank Credit Sales	J41		124 65	1558 17				1682 82
2	15	Mike Antonello	J41	97 12						97 12
3	16	Cash Sales	J41		41 54	519 27				546 81
4	16	Bank Credit Sales	J41		149 00	1862 51				2011 51
5	17	Cash Sales	J42		228 25	2853 19				3081 44
6	17	Bank Credit Sales	J42		7 08	98 47				79 55
7	17	Terry Alenikov	J42	75 12						2875 92
8	18	Cash Sales	J42		238 46	2980 15				3218 56
9	19	Cash Sales	J42		181 06	2263 20				2444 26
10	19	Bank Credit Sales	J42		72 97	912 16				985 13
11	20	Cash Sales	J42		210 41	2630 08				2840 49
12	20	Bank Credit Sales	J42		158 72	1984 03				2142 75
13	21	Cash Sales	J43		67 10	838 68				905 78
14	21	Bank Credit Sales	J43		290 17	3627 14				3917 31
15				7072 98	4820 76	60259 43				72153 17
16	22	Cash Sales	J44		56 52	706 49				763 01
17	22	Bank Credit Sales	J44		81 67	1020 94				1102 61
18	22	Kathy Oh	J44	169 21						169 21
19	23	Cash Sales	J44		119 43	1492 90				1612 33
20	23	Bank Credit Sales	J44		39 95	499 30				539 25
21	24	Cash Sales	J45		4 55	56 88				61 43
22	24	Bank Credit Sales	J45		83 06	1038 27				1121 33
23	24	Monica Mooney	J45	52 76						52 76
24	26	Cash Sales	J45		170 91	2136 32				2307 23
25	26	Bank Credit Sales	J45		331 76	4144 99				4478 75
26	26	D. Gutierrez	J45	448 54						448 54
27	27	Cash Sales	J45		337 10	4213 72				4550 82
28	27	Bank Credit Sales	J45		271 43	3392 81				3664 24
29	27	Dahaal Howard	J45	127 50						127 50
30	28	Cash Sales	J46		415 96	5199 52				5615 48
31	28	Bank Credit Sales	J46		166 20	2002 55				2162 75
32	29	Sales	J46		169 01	2112 69				2281 70
33	29	Gia Marakas	J46	999 00						999 00
34	29	M. Miller	J46	950 94						950 94
35	30	Sales	J46		425 25	5315 61				5740 86
36	30	Jean Kim	J46	3195 49						3195 49
37	31	Sales	J46		114 17	1427 06				1541 23
				13016.42	7601.73	95021.48				115,639.63
				(111)	(231)	(401)				(101)

41,611.84

22,605.95

13016.42

Home Team Advantage Practice Set

61

Name_____ Date_____ Class_____

CASH PAYMENTS JOURNAL

PAGE___35___

	DATE	CK. NO.	PAYEE	POST REF	ACCOUNTS PAYABLE DEBIT	OTHER ACCOUNTS DEBIT — ACCT. NAME	POST REF	AMOUNT	PURCHASES DISCOUNT CREDIT	CASH CREDIT	
	2013										
1	Dec 1	609	Archival Card Stor	J35	650 00					650 00	
2	2	610	Dept. of Power	J35		Utilities	641	524 79		524 79	
3	2	611	Grand Prairie Mgmt	J35		Rent	613	2500 00		2500 00	
4	3	612	Prism Insurance	J35		Ins. Exp.	607	1340 00		1340 00	
5	4	613	Tyler Disp. Serv.	J35		Rubbish Exp	614	300 00		300 00	
6	4	614	Sports Authentica	J35	5000 00					5000 00	
7	5	615	First Bank of Texas	J35		Payroll Tax E	612	3204 00		3204 00	
8	5	616	Dallas Teleph.	J35		Telecom. Exp	633	163 00		163 00	
9					5656 00			8031 79		13681 79	
10	8	617	Texas Racing Assoc.	J38		Tradeshow	634	2000 00		2000 00	
11	8	618	Duong's Jersey Outlet	J38	12058 50					12058 50	
12	8	619	Sentinal Alarms	J38		Security Exp	631	99 00		99 00	
13	9	620	Woodworks, Inc	J38	750 00	Purchases Disc.		15 00	15 00	735 00	-15
14	9	621	Intl. Sports Supp.	J38	3200 00	Purchase Disc.		64 00	64 00	3136 00	-64
15	9	622	Texas Dept. of Rev.	J39		Payroll Tax E.	612	9222 50		9222 50	
16	10	623	Office Staples	J39		Office Supplies	135	253 21		253 21	
17	12	624	Office Staples	J40		Office Supplies	135	45 23		45 23	
18	12	625	U.S. Post Office	J40		Office Sup.	135	78 00		78 00	
19					21579 50			19929 73	79 00	41388 23	
20	15	626	Payroll	J41		Salaries Pay	205	8720 08		8720 08	
21	15	627	Woodworks, Inc	J41	450 00	Purchase Disc.		9 00	9 00	441 00	-9
22	15	628	Autograph Central	J41	2000 00	Purchase Disc.		40 00	40 00	1960 00	-40
23	16	629	Lone Star Hockey Cl.	J42		Advertising	601	2000 00		2000 00	
24	16	630	Calderon Sports	J42	800 00	Purchase Disc.		40 00	40 00	760 00	(-40)
25	17	631	Ground Delivery	J42		Freight-In	506	122 32		122 32	
26	18	632	Dallas Digi. Net.	J42		Telecom. Exp	633	399 99		399 99	
27	19	633	First Bank of Texas	J43		Payroll Tax E	612	3204 00		3204 00	
28	19	634	Bracket Sports Col	J43		Adv. Exp	661	1000 00		1000 00	
29					24740 50			35211 64	128 00	60084 54	
30	22	635	Catalog Master	J44		Adv. Exp	601	1200 00		1200 00	
31	22	636	Dallas Softball Leag	J44		Adv. Exp.	601	500 00		500 00	
32	23	637	Ground Delivery	J44		Freight-In	506	234 00		234 00	
33	23	638	Ron Morris	J44		Trade Show	634	158 00		158 00	
34	24	639	Bell Security	J45		Security Ex	632	249 99		249 99	
35	26	640	Sports Authentica	J45	1000 00					1000 00	
36	26	641	Ground Delivery	J45		Freight-In	506	512 00		512 00	
37	30	642	Ringside Enter.	J46	600 00				12 00	588 00	-12

Home Team Advantage Practice Set

Copyright © 2007 The McGraw-Hill Companies

CASH PAYMENTS JOURNAL   PAGE 34

	DATE	CK. NO.	PAYEE	POST REF	ACCOUNTS PAYABLE DEBIT	OTHER ACCOUNTS DEBIT			PURCHASES DISCOUNT CREDIT	CASH CREDIT
						ACCT. NAME	POST REF	AMOUNT		
	Dec 30	643	Sports Authentica	J46	500 00					500 00
1	31	644	Dan Morris	J46		Withdrawal	302	4000 00		4000 00
2	31		Bank Credit Discount	J47		C.C. Discount	602	259 66		259 66
3	31	645	Payroll	J47		Salaries P	205	6183 00		6183 00
4					26 828 50			4851 2 69	140 00	75 481 19
5					27 008 50			4851 2 69	180 00	75 301 19
6										
7					(202)				(553)	(101)
8										
9										
10										
11										
12										
13										
14										
15										
16										
17										
18										
19										
20										
21										
22										
23										
24										
25										
26										
27										
28										
29										
30										
31										
32										
33										
34										
35										
36										
37										

PURCHASES JOURNAL

PAGE ___35___

	DATE	PURCHASED FROM	INVOICE NO.	INVOICE DATE	TERMS	POST REF	PURCHASES DR ACCTS PAYABLE CR	
1	2013							1
2	Dec 1	Duong's Jersey Outlet	608	11/29/12	N/30	J37	1205850	2
3	3	Woodworks, Inc.	2932	12/01/12	2/10, N/30	J38	25000	3
4	9	Autograph Central	2341	12/8/12	2/10, N/30		1286850	4
5	9	Autograph Central	2341	12/8/12	2/10, N/30	J39	200000	5
6	10	Sports Authentica	123	12/7/12	N/30	J39	100000	6
7	11	Calderon Sports Supply	421	12/8/12	5/10, N/30	J39	80000	7
8	11	Woodworks, Inc	2967	12/8/12	2/10, N/30	J39	45000	8
9	16	Sports Authentica	197	12/16/12	N/30		1705850	9
10	16	Sports Authentica	197	12/16/12	N/30	J42	50000	10 1755850
11	22	Ringside Entertainment	6291	12/20/12	2/10, N/30	J44	60000	11
12	24	Toy warehouse	2532	12/22/12	N/30	J44	240000	12
13	24	Worldwide Tennis	5213	12/23/12	2/10, N/30	J45	30000	13
14	30	Int'l Sports Supplies	6982	12/26/12	2/10, N/30	J46	120050	14 22058.60
15							2205850	15
16								16
17							(501/202)	17
18								18
19								19
20								20
21								21
22								22
23								23
24								24
25								25
26								26
27								27
28								28
29								29
30								30
31								31
32								32
33								33
34								34
35								35
36								36
37								37
38								38

Home Team Advantage Practice Set

Name_____ Date_____ Class_____

GENERAL JOURNAL

PAGE ___35___

	DATE	DESCRIPTION	POST REF.	DEBIT	CREDIT	
1						1
2						2
3						3
4						4
5						5
6						6
7						7
8						8
9						9
10						10
11						11
12						12
13						13
14						14
15						15
16						16
17						17
18						18
19						19
20						20
21						21
22						22
23						23
24						24
25						25
26						26
27						27
28						28
29						29
30						30
31						31
32						32
33						33
34						34
35						35
36						36
37						37
38						38

Home Team Advantage Practice Set

	DATE	DESCRIPTION	POST REF.	DEBIT	CREDIT	
1	2006					1
2	Dec 1	Cash	CR35	623 71		2
3		Sales	CR35		577 51	3
4		Sales Tax Payable	CR35		46 20	4
5		to record cash sales				5
6						6
7	1	Cash	CR35	1281 25		7
8		Sales			1186 34	8
9		Sales Tax Payable			94 91	9
10		To record bank credit card sales				10
11						11
12	1	Cash		72 15		12
13		Accounts Receivable			72 15	13
14		to record payment from Steve Carlyle				14
15		on account				15
16						16
17	2	Cash		1550 60		17
18		Sales			1435 74	18
19		Sales Tax Payable			114 86	19
20		to record cash sales				20
21						21
22	2	Cash		331 69		22
23		Sales			307 12	23
24		Sales Tax Payable			24 57	24
25		to record bank credit card sales				25
26						26
27	2	Cash		1847 56		27
28		Accounts Receivable			1847 56	28
29		payment from Rick Marquez on				29
30		account				30
31						31
32	3	Cash		1377 19		32
33		Sales			1275 18	33
34		Sales Tax Payable			102 01	34
35						35
36	3	Cash		1559 11		36
37		Sales			1443 62	37
38		Sales Tax Payable			115 49	38

Home Team Advantage Practice Set Copyright © 2007 The McGraw-Hill Companies

Name_____ Date_____ Class_____

GENERAL JOURNAL

PAGE 36

	DATE	DESCRIPTION	POST REF.	DEBIT	CREDIT	
1	2013	Cash		487 22		1
2	Dec 3	Cash [Accounts Receivable]		487 22	487 22	2
3		Accounts Receivable			487 22	3
4						4
5	4	Cash		1239 01		5
6		Sales			1147 23	6
7		Sales Tax Payable			91 78	7
8						8
9	4	Cash		230 51		9
10		Sales			213 44	10
11		Sales Tax Payable			17 07	11
12						12
13	4	Cash		1500 00		13
14		Accounts Receivable			1500 00	14
15						15
16	5	Cash		3428 21		16
17		Sales			3174 27	17
18		Sales Tax Payable			253 94	18
19						19
20	6	Cash		1139 50		20
21		Sales			1055 09	21
22		Sales Tax Payable			84 41	22
23						23
24	6	Cash		3343 82		24
25		Sales			3096 13	25
26		Sales Tax Payable			247 69	26
27						27
28	7	Cash		4095 62		28
29		Sales			3792 24	29
30		Sales Tax Payable			303 38	30
31						31
32	7	Cash		137 47		32
33		Accounts Receivable			137 47	33
34		payment on account for David Jordan				34
35						35
36	7	Cash		282 13		36
37		Accounts Receivable			282 13	37
38		payment on account for Kristen Boucher				38

Home Team Advantage Practice Set

Name_____ Date_____ Class_____

GENERAL JOURNAL
PAGE __37__

	DATE		DESCRIPTION	POST REF.	DEBIT	CREDIT	
1	2013						1
2	Dec	1	Accounts Payable		650 00		2
3			Cash			650 00	3
4			issued check 609 payable to Archival				4
5			card storage supplies on account				5
6							6
7		2	Utilities Expense		524 79		7
8			Cash			524 79	8
9			issued check 610 to Dept. of Power				9
10							10
11		2	Rent Expense		2500 00		11
12			Cash			2500 00	12
13			issued check 611 to Grand Prairie Prop. Mgmt				13
14							14
15		3	Insurance Expense		1340 00		15
16			Cash			1340 00	16
17			Issued check 612 to Prism Insurance				17
18							18
19		4	Rubbish Removal Expense		360 00		19
20			Cash			300 00	20
21			issued check 613 to Tyler Disposal Service				21
22							22
23		4	Accounts Payable		5000 00		23
24			Cash			5000 00	24
25			issued check 614 to Sports Authentication				25
26							26
27		5	Payroll Tax Expense		3204 00		27
28			Cash			3204 00	28
29			issued check 615 to Bank of Texas				29
30							30
31		5	Telecommunication Expense		163 00		31
32			Cash			163 00	32
33			issued check 616 to Dallas Telephone				33
34							34
35		1	Purchases		12058 50		35
36			Accounts Payable			12058 50	36
37			purchased from Duong's Jersey Outlet				37
38			invoice # 608				38

68 **Home Team Advantage Practice Set**   Copyright © 2007 The McGraw-Hill Companies

GENERAL JOURNAL

	DATE		DESCRIPTION	POST REF.	DEBIT	CREDIT	
1	2006						1
2	Dec	3	Store Fixtures and Equipment		750 00		2
3			Accounts Payable			750 00	3
4			purchased on account from woodwork's				4
5			inc. invoice # 2932				5
6							6
7		10	Sales Returns and Allowances		40 00		7
8			Accounts Receivable			40 00	8
9			issued credit memo. 89 to Monica				9
10			Mooney for damaged merchandise				10
11							11
12		8	Cash		2023 19		12
13			sales			1873 32	13
14			Sale Tax Payable			149 87	14
15			to record cash & bank credit sales				15
16							16
17		8	Cash		500 33		17
18			Accounts Receivable			520 33	18
19							19
20		8	Accounts Receivable		58 44		20
21			Sales			54 11	21
22			sale Tax Payable			4 33	22
23							23
24		8	Trade Show Expense		2000 00		24
25			Cash			2000 00	25
26							26
27		8	Accounts Payable – Duong's Jersey Outlet		1205 850		27
28			Cash			1205 850	28
29							29
30		8	Security Expense		99 00		30
31			Cash			99 00	31
32							32
33		9	Cash		2174 12		33
34			Sales			2013 07	34
35			Sales Tax Payable			161 05	35
36							36
37		9	Accounts Payable – Int'l. Sports Supply		3200 00		37
38			Purchase Discount Expense		00	64 00	38
			Cash			3 2 36 00	

GENERAL JOURNAL

PAGE _39_

	DATE		DESCRIPTION	POST REF.	DEBIT	CREDIT	
1	2013						1
2	Dec	9	Accounts Payable - Woodworks, Inc.		3 75000		2
3			Purchase Discount Expense			7 1500	3
4			Cash Discount Expense			7 3500	4
5							5
6		9	Payroll Tax Expense		9 22250		6
7			Cash			9 22250	7
8							8
9		9	Purchases		2 00000		9
10			Accounts Payable			2 00000	10
11							11
12		10	Cash		1 59285		12
13			Sales			1 47486	13
14			Sales Tax Payable			1 1799	14
15							15
16		10	Cash		7 2150		16
17			Accounts Receivable			7 2150	17
18							18
19		10	Office Supplies		2 5321		19
20			Cash			2 5321	20
21							21
22		10	Purchases		1 00000		22
23			Accounts Payable			1 00000	23
24							24
25		11	Cash		2 26421		25
26			Sales			2 09649	26
27			Sales Tax Payable			1 6772	27
28							28
29		11	Cash		9 5000		29
30			Accounts Receivable			9 5000	30
31							31
32		11	Purchases		8 0000		32
33			Accounts Payable			8 0000	33
34							34
35		11	Store Fixtures and Equipment		4 5000		35
36			Accounts Payable			4 5000	36
37							37
38							38

General Ledger

HOME TEAM ADVANTAGE
CHART OF ACCOUNTS

ASSETS

101	Cash
103	Petty Cash Fund
111	Accounts Receivable
112	Allowance for Doubtful Accounts
113	Interest Receivable
114	Short-Term Investments
115	Security Deposits
121	Merchandise Inventory
131	Prepaid Insurance
133	Store Supplies
135	Office Supplies
145	Store Fixtures and Equipment
146	Accumulated Depreciation – Store Fixtures and Equipment

LIABILITIES

202	Accounts Payable
205	Salaries Payable
221	Social Security Tax Payable
222	Medicare Tax Payable
223	Employee Income Tax Payable
226	Payroll Taxes Payable
231	Sales Tax Payable

OWNER'S EQUITY

301	Dan Morris, Capital
302	Dan Morris, Drawing
399	Income Summary

REVENUE

401	Sales
441	Sales Returns and Allowances
491	Interest Income

EXPENSES

501	Purchases
506	Freight in
551	Purchases Returns and Allowances
553	Purchases Discount
601	Advertising Expense
602	Credit Card Discount Expense
603	Depreciation Expense
607	Insurance Expense
611	Office Supplies Expense
612	Payroll Taxes Expense
613	Rent Expense
614	Rubbish Removal Expense
621	Salaries Expense – Office
622	Salaries Expense – Sales
623	Salaries Expense – Stockroom
631	Security Expense
632	Store Supplies Expense
633	Telecommunications Expense
634	Trade Show Expense
635	Uncollectible Accounts Expense
641	Utilities Expense

ACCOUNT Cash   **ACCOUNT NO.** ___101___

DATE		DESCRIPTION	POST REF.	DEBIT	CREDIT	BALANCE	
						DEBIT	CREDIT
2006							
Dec.	1	Balance	✓			37 1 2 1 96	
	31		CR36	115 63 9 63			
	31		CP36		75 30 1 19		

ACCOUNT Petty Cash Fund   **ACCOUNT NO.** ___103___

DATE		DESCRIPTION	POST REF.	DEBIT	CREDIT	BALANCE	
						DEBIT	CREDIT
2006							
Dec.	1	Balance	✓			5 0 00	

ACCOUNT Accounts Receivable   **ACCOUNT NO.** ___111___

DATE		DESCRIPTION	POST REF.	DEBIT	CREDIT	BALANCE	
						DEBIT	CREDIT
2006							
Dec.	1	Balance	✓			14 5 3 2 45	
	31		S)35	17 9 2 7 33		32 4 5 9 78	
	31		CR36		13 0 1 6 42	19 4 4 3 36	

ACCOUNT Allowance for Doubtful Accounts   **ACCOUNT NO.** ___112___

DATE		DESCRIPTION	POST REF.	DEBIT	CREDIT	BALANCE	
						DEBIT	CREDIT
2006							
Dec.	1	Balance	✓				5 9 5 43

Name_____ Date_____ Class_____

ACCOUNT   Interest Receivable   ACCOUNT NO. ___113___

DATE		DESCRIPTION	POST REF.	DEBIT	CREDIT	BALANCE	
						DEBIT	CREDIT

ACCOUNT   Short-Term Investments   ACCOUNT NO. ___114___

DATE		DESCRIPTION	POST REF.	DEBIT	CREDIT	BALANCE	
						DEBIT	CREDIT
2006							
Dec.	1	Balance	✓			35 0 0 0 00	

ACCOUNT   Security Deposits   ACCOUNT NO. ___115___

DATE		DESCRIPTION	POST REF.	DEBIT	CREDIT	BALANCE	
						DEBIT	CREDIT
2006							
Dec.	1	Balance	✓			5 0 0 00	

ACCOUNT   Merchandise Inventory   ACCOUNT NO. ___121___

DATE		DESCRIPTION	POST REF.	DEBIT	CREDIT	BALANCE	
						DEBIT	CREDIT
2006							
Dec.	1	Balance	✓			198 2 2 1 75	

ACCOUNT   Prepaid Insurance   **ACCOUNT NO.**   131

DATE		DESCRIPTION	POST REF.	DEBIT	CREDIT	BALANCE	
						DEBIT	CREDIT
2006							
Dec.	1	Balance	✓			5 7 8 0 00	

ACCOUNT   Store Supplies   **ACCOUNT NO.**   133

DATE		DESCRIPTION	POST REF.	DEBIT	CREDIT	BALANCE	
						DEBIT	CREDIT
2006							
Dec.	1	Balance	✓			2 2 1 0 00	

ACCOUNT   Office Supplies   **ACCOUNT NO.**   135

DATE		DESCRIPTION	POST REF.	DEBIT	CREDIT	BALANCE	
						DEBIT	CREDIT
2006							
Dec.	1	Balance	✓			3 9 8 2 76	
	10			2 5 3 21		4 2 3 5 97	
	12			4 5 23		4 2 8 1 20	
	12			7 8 00		4 3 5 9 20	

ACCOUNT   Store Fixtures and Equipment   **ACCOUNT NO.**   145

DATE		DESCRIPTION	POST REF.	DEBIT	CREDIT	BALANCE	
						DEBIT	CREDIT
2006							
Dec.	1	Balance	✓			36 4 0 0 00	

ACCOUNT Accumulated Depreciation - Store Fixtures and Equipment   **ACCOUNT NO.**   146

DATE		DESCRIPTION	POST REF.	DEBIT	CREDIT	BALANCE DEBIT	BALANCE CREDIT
2006							
Dec.	1	Balance	✓				6 5 5 2 00

ACCOUNT Accounts Payable   **ACCOUNT NO.**   202

DATE		DESCRIPTION	POST REF.	DEBIT	CREDIT	BALANCE DEBIT	BALANCE CREDIT
2006							
Dec.	1	Balance	✓				9 8 5 0 00
	31		CP36	27 0 0 8 00		17 1 5 8 00	
	31		PJ35	22 0 5 8 50	22 0 5 8 50		4 9 0 0 50

ACCOUNT Salaries Payable   **ACCOUNT NO.**   205

DATE		DESCRIPTION	POST REF.	DEBIT	CREDIT	BALANCE DEBIT	BALANCE CREDIT
2006							
Dec	15			8 7 2 0 00		8 7 2 0 00	
	31			6 1 8 3 00		14 9 0 3 00	

ACCOUNT Social Security Tax Payable   **ACCOUNT NO.**   221

DATE		DESCRIPTION	POST REF.	DEBIT	CREDIT	BALANCE DEBIT	BALANCE CREDIT
2006							
Dec.	1	Balance	✓				5 4 1 00

ACCOUNT Medicare Tax Payable _____ **ACCOUNT NO.** 222

DATE		DESCRIPTION	POST REF.	DEBIT	CREDIT	BALANCE	
						DEBIT	CREDIT
2006							
Dec.	1	Balance	✓				1 2 6 00

ACCOUNT Employee Income Tax Payable _____ **ACCOUNT NO.** 223

DATE		DESCRIPTION	POST REF.	DEBIT	CREDIT	BALANCE	
						DEBIT	CREDIT
2006							
Dec.	1	Balance	✓				1 8 7 0 00

ACCOUNT Payroll Taxes Payable _____ **ACCOUNT NO.** 226

DATE		DESCRIPTION	POST REF.	DEBIT	CREDIT	BALANCE	
						DEBIT	CREDIT
2006							
Dec.	1	Balance	✓				6 6 7 00
	5			3 2 0 4 50			
	9	Texas Dept. of Rev.		9 2 2 50			
	19			3 2 0 4 50			

ACCOUNT Sales Tax Payable _____ **ACCOUNT NO.** 231

DATE		DESCRIPTION	POST REF.	DEBIT	CREDIT	BALANCE	
						DEBIT	CREDIT
2006							
Dec.	1	Balance	✓				9 2 2 2 50
	31		SJ35		13 2 7 9 94		
	31		CR36		7 6 0 1 73		

ACCOUNT Dan Morris, Capital   **ACCOUNT NO.** 301

DATE		DESCRIPTION	POST REF.	DEBIT	CREDIT	BALANCE DEBIT	BALANCE CREDIT
2006							
Dec.	1	Balance	✓				301 3 2 5 38

ACCOUNT Dan Morris, Drawing   **ACCOUNT NO.** 302

DATE		DESCRIPTION	POST REF.	DEBIT	CREDIT	BALANCE DEBIT	BALANCE CREDIT
2006							
Dec.	1	Balance	✓			44 0 0 0 00	
	31			4 0 0 0 00		48 0 0 0 00	

ACCOUNT Income Summary   **ACCOUNT NO.** 399

DATE	DESCRIPTION	POST REF.	DEBIT	CREDIT	BALANCE DEBIT	BALANCE CREDIT

ACCOUNT Sales   **ACCOUNT NO.** 401

DATE		DESCRIPTION	POST REF.	DEBIT	CREDIT	BALANCE DEBIT	BALANCE CREDIT
2006							
Dec.	1	Balance	✓				914 6 6 0 33
	31		SJ35		16 5 9 9 39		
	31		CR36		95 0 2 1 48		

ACCOUNT Sales Returns and Allowances   **ACCOUNT NO.** 441

DATE		DESCRIPTION	POST REF.	DEBIT	CREDIT	BALANCE DEBIT	BALANCE CREDIT
2006							
Dec.	1	Balance	✓			15 0 9 2 85	

ACCOUNT Interest Income   **ACCOUNT NO.** 491

DATE		DESCRIPTION	POST REF.	DEBIT	CREDIT	BALANCE DEBIT	BALANCE CREDIT

ACCOUNT Purchases   **ACCOUNT NO.** 501

DATE		DESCRIPTION	POST REF.	DEBIT	CREDIT	BALANCE DEBIT	BALANCE CREDIT
2006							
Dec.	1	Balance	✓			582 3 6 2 64	
	31		CP35	22 0 5 8 50			

ACCOUNT Freight In   **ACCOUNT NO.** 506

DATE		DESCRIPTION	POST REF.	DEBIT	CREDIT	BALANCE DEBIT	BALANCE CREDIT
2006							
Dec.	1	Balance	✓			16 1 5 6 52	
	17	Ground Delivery		1 2 2 32			
	23			2 3 4 06			
	26			5 1 2 00			

ACCOUNT Purchases Returns and Allowances   **ACCOUNT NO.** 551

DATE		DESCRIPTION	POST REF.	DEBIT	CREDIT	BALANCE DEBIT	BALANCE CREDIT
2006							
Dec.	1	Balance	✓				8 9 6 5 73

ACCOUNT Purchases Discount   **ACCOUNT NO.** 553

DATE		DESCRIPTION	POST REF.	DEBIT	CREDIT	BALANCE DEBIT	BALANCE CREDIT
2006							
Dec.	1	Balance	✓				4 2 9 1 52
	31		CP36		1 80 00		4 47 1 52

ACCOUNT Advertising Expense   **ACCOUNT NO.** 601

DATE		DESCRIPTION	POST REF.	DEBIT	CREDIT	BALANCE DEBIT	BALANCE CREDIT
2006							
Dec.	1	Balance	✓			3 6 0 0 00	
	16	Lone Star Hockey Assoc.		2 0 0 0 00		5 6 0 0 00	
	19			1 0 0 0 00			
	22			1 2 0 0 00			
	22			5 0 0 00			

ACCOUNT Credit Card Discount Expense   **ACCOUNT NO.** 602

DATE		DESCRIPTION	POST REF.	DEBIT	CREDIT	BALANCE DEBIT	BALANCE CREDIT
2006							
Dec.	1	Balance	✓			2 3 2 1 88	
	31			2 59 66			

Name_____ Date_____ Class_____

ACCOUNT Depreciation Expense
ACCOUNT NO. 603

DATE	DESCRIPTION	POST REF.	DEBIT	CREDIT	BALANCE DEBIT	BALANCE CREDIT

ACCOUNT Insurance Expense
ACCOUNT NO. 607

DATE	DESCRIPTION	POST REF.	DEBIT	CREDIT	BALANCE DEBIT	BALANCE CREDIT
2006						
Dec 3			1 34 0 00		1 34 0 00	

ACCOUNT Office Supplies Expense
ACCOUNT NO. 611

DATE	DESCRIPTION	POST REF.	DEBIT	CREDIT	BALANCE DEBIT	BALANCE CREDIT

ACCOUNT Payroll Taxes Expense
ACCOUNT NO. 612

DATE	DESCRIPTION	POST REF.	DEBIT	CREDIT	BALANCE DEBIT	BALANCE CREDIT
2006						
Dec. 1	Balance	✓			14 6 7 4 00	
5			3 2 0 4 00		17 8 7 8 00	
9	Texas Dept. of Revenue		9 2 2 2 50		27 1 0 0 50	
19			3 2 0 4 00		30 3 0 4 50	

82 **Home Team Advantage Practice Set** Copyright © 2007 The McGraw-Hill Companies

Name_____ Date_____ Class_____

ACCOUNT   Rent Expense

ACCOUNT NO.   613

DATE		DESCRIPTION	POST REF.	DEBIT	CREDIT	BALANCE DEBIT	BALANCE CREDIT
2006							
Dec.	1	Balance	✓			26 4 0 0 00	
	2	December rent		250000		2890000	

ACCOUNT   Rubbish Removal Expense

ACCOUNT NO.   614

DATE		DESCRIPTION	POST REF.	DEBIT	CREDIT	BALANCE DEBIT	BALANCE CREDIT
2006							
Dec.	1	Balance	✓			3 3 0 0 00	
	4			30000		360000	

ACCOUNT   Salaries Expense - Office

ACCOUNT NO.   621

DATE		DESCRIPTION	POST REF.	DEBIT	CREDIT	BALANCE DEBIT	BALANCE CREDIT
2006							
Dec.	1	Balance	✓			95 0 4 0 00	

ACCOUNT   Salaries Expense - Sales

ACCOUNT NO.   622

DATE		DESCRIPTION	POST REF.	DEBIT	CREDIT	BALANCE DEBIT	BALANCE CREDIT
2006							
Dec.	1	Balance	✓			71 2 8 0 00	

Name_____ Date_____ Class_____

ACCOUNT Salaries Expense - Stockroom ACCOUNT NO. 623

DATE		DESCRIPTION	POST REF.	DEBIT	CREDIT	BALANCE	
						DEBIT	CREDIT
2006							
Dec	1	Balance	✓			25 5 2 0 00	

ACCOUNT Security Expense ACCOUNT NO. 631

DATE		DESCRIPTION	POST REF.	DEBIT	CREDIT	BALANCE	
						DEBIT	CREDIT
2006							
Dec.	1	Balance	✓			3 8 3 8 89	
	8	Sentinal Alarms		9 9 00		3 9 3 7 89	
	24	Bell Security		2 4 9 99		4 1 8 7 88	

ACCOUNT Store Supplies Expense ACCOUNT NO. 632

DATE		DESCRIPTION	POST REF.	DEBIT	CREDIT	BALANCE	
						DEBIT	CREDIT

ACCOUNT Telecommunications Expense ACCOUNT NO. 633

DATE		DESCRIPTION	POST REF.	DEBIT	CREDIT	BALANCE	
						DEBIT	CREDIT
2006							
Dec.	1	Balance	✓			6 0 7 5 48	
	5			1 6 3 00		6 2 3 8 48	
	18			3 9 9 99		6 6 3 8 47	

Name_____ Date_____ Class_____

ACCOUNT Trade Show Expense   ACCOUNT NO.   634

DATE		DESCRIPTION	POST REF.	DEBIT	CREDIT	BALANCE DEBIT	BALANCE CREDIT
2006							
Dec.	1	Balance	✓			3 6 2 2 00	
	8	Texas Racing Assoc.		2 0 0 0 00		5 6 2 2 00	
	23	Ron Morris		1 5 8 00		5 7 8 0 00	

ACCOUNT Uncollectible Accounts Expense   ACCOUNT NO.   635

DATE	DESCRIPTION	POST REF.	DEBIT	CREDIT	BALANCE DEBIT	BALANCE CREDIT

ACCOUNT Utilities Expense   ACCOUNT NO.   641

DATE		DESCRIPTION	POST REF.	DEBIT	CREDIT	BALANCE DEBIT	BALANCE CREDIT
2006							
Dec.	1	Balance	✓			11 5 8 3 71	
	2	paid bill		5 2 4 79		12 1 0 8 50	

Home Team Advantage Practice Set

Accounts Receivable Ledger

ACCOUNTS RECEIVABLE LEDGER
CHARGE ACCOUNT CUSTOMERS

Number	Customer Account Customer Name
1089	Rick Marquez
2369	Steve Carlyle
2745	Michelle Weinstein
2984	Jamaal Howard
3118	Dave Jordan
4277	Kristen Boucher
4316	Laurie Chapman
5081	Brad Smythe
5748	Terri Alenikov
6281	Gia Marakas
6443	Wendy Gau
6770	Marques Miller
6846	Jean Kim
6907	Ann Roff
7651	Mike Antonello
7649	Linda Padilla
7805	Kathy Oh
9623	Jeff Briggs
9672	Monica Mooney
9864	Debbie Gutierrez

ACCOUNT   Terri Alenikov   ACCOUNT NO.   5748

DATE		DESCRIPTION	POST REF.	DEBIT	CREDIT	BALANCE
2006						
Dec.	1	Balance	✓			7 5 12
	8	Purchase		58 44		1 33 56
	17	Payment			75 12	58 44

ACCOUNT   Mike Antonello   ACCOUNT NO.   7651

DATE		DESCRIPTION	POST REF.	DEBIT	CREDIT	BALANCE
2006						
Dec.	1	Balance	✓			9 7 12
	15	Payment			97 12	-0-
	20	purchase		3 47 97		3 47 97

ACCOUNT   Jeff Briggs   ACCOUNT NO.   9623

DATE		DESCRIPTION	POST REF.	DEBIT	CREDIT	BALANCE
2006						
Dec	5	purchase		76 50		76 50

ACCOUNT Kristen Boucher   **ACCOUNT NO.** 4277

DATE		DESCRIPTION	POST REF.	DEBIT	CREDIT	BALANCE
2006						
Dec.	1	Balance	✓			2 8 2 13
	7	Payment			2 8 2 13	←
	15	Purchase		6 6 5 09		6 6 5 09

ACCOUNT Steve Carlyle   **ACCOUNT NO.** 2369

DATE		DESCRIPTION	POST REF.	DEBIT	CREDIT	BALANCE
2006						
Dec.	1	Balance	✓			7 2 15
	1	Paid Balance			7 2 15	←
	7	Purchase		4 5 3 6 88		4 5 3 6 88
	11	Payment			9 5 0 00	3 5 8 6 88

ACCOUNT Laurie Chapman   **ACCOUNT NO.** 4316

DATE		DESCRIPTION	POST REF.	DEBIT	CREDIT	BALANCE
2006						
Dec.	1	Balance	✓			2 2 6 1 07
	4	Payment			1 5 0 0 00	7 6 1 07
	23	Purchase		7 8 1 08		1 5 4 2 15

Name_____ Date_____ Class_____

ACCOUNT Wendy Gau   **ACCOUNT NO.**   6443

DATE		DESCRIPTION	POST REF.	DEBIT	CREDIT	BALANCE
2006						
Dec.	1	Balance	✓			7 2 1 50
	10	Payment	SJ35		721 50	0
	19	Purchase		770 31		770 31

ACCOUNT Debbie Gutierrez   **ACCOUNT NO.**   9864

DATE		DESCRIPTION	POST REF.	DEBIT	CREDIT	BALANCE
2006						
Dec.	1	Balance	✓			4 4 8 54
	26	purchase		676 64		1125 18
	26	payment			448 54	676 64

ACCOUNT Jamaal Howard   **ACCOUNT NO.**   2984

DATE		DESCRIPTION	POST REF.	DEBIT	CREDIT	BALANCE
2006						
Dec	1	made a purchase	SJ35	127 50		127 50
	27	Payment			127 50	0

92   **Home Team Advantage Practice Set**   Copyright © 2007 The McGraw-Hill Companies

Name_____ Date_____ Class_____

ACCOUNT Dave Jordan   **ACCOUNT NO.** 3118

DATE		DESCRIPTION	POST REF.	DEBIT	CREDIT	BALANCE
2006						
Dec.	1	Balance	✓			1 3 7 47
	7	Payment	SJ36		137 47	0
	14	Purchase	SJ35	1992 19		1 992 19

ACCOUNT Jean Kim   **ACCOUNT NO.** 6846

DATE		DESCRIPTION	POST REF.	DEBIT	CREDIT	BALANCE
2006						
Dec.	1	Balance	✓			3 1 9 5 49
	30	Payment			3195 49	0

ACCOUNT Gia Marakas   **ACCOUNT NO.** 6281

DATE		DESCRIPTION	POST REF.	DEBIT	CREDIT	BALANCE
2006						
Dec	2	purchase	SJ35	999 00		999 00
	29	payment			999 00	0

Name_____ Date_____ Class_____

ACCOUNT Rick Marquez _____ **ACCOUNT NO.** 1089

DATE		DESCRIPTION	POST REF.	DEBIT	CREDIT	BALANCE
2006						
Dec.	1	Balance	✓			1 5 4 7 06
	2	Payment	SJ35		1 5 4 7 06	0
	7	Purchase	SJ35	4 3 7 75		4 3 7 75

ACCOUNT Marques Miller _____ **ACCOUNT NO.** 6770

DATE		DESCRIPTION	POST REF.	DEBIT	CREDIT	BALANCE
2006						
Dec	3	Purchase	SJ35		9 50 94	9 50 94
	29	payment		9 50 94		0

ACCOUNT Monica Mooney _____ **ACCOUNT NO.** 9672

DATE		DESCRIPTION	POST REF.	DEBIT	CREDIT	BALANCE
2006						
Dec.	1	Balance	✓			5 2 76
	5	Purchase	SJ35	4 56 88		5 09 64
	24	payment			52 76	4 56 88

ACCOUNT Kathy Oh   **ACCOUNT NO.** 7805

DATE		DESCRIPTION	POST REF.	DEBIT	CREDIT	BALANCE
2006						
Dec.	1	Balance	✓			1 6 9 21
	17	Purchase		1 9 1 34		3 6 0 55
	22	Payment			1 6 9 21	1 9 1 34

ACCOUNT Linda Padilla   **ACCOUNT NO.** 7649

DATE		DESCRIPTION	POST REF.	DEBIT	CREDIT	BALANCE
2006						
Dec.	1	Balance	✓			3 7 8 2 40
	22	Purchase		5 6 0 38		4 3 2 78

ACCOUNT Ann Roff   **ACCOUNT NO.** 6907

DATE		DESCRIPTION	POST REF.	DEBIT	CREDIT	BALANCE
2006						
Dec.	1	Balance	✓			7 0 2 88
	13	Purchase	SJ35	6 5 8 75		1 3 6 1 63
	14	Payment			7 0 2 88	6 5 8 75

Home Team Advantage Practice Set

Name_____ Date_____ Class_____

ACCOUNT Brad Smythe   **ACCOUNT NO.** 5081

DATE		DESCRIPTION	POST REF.	DEBIT	CREDIT	BALANCE
2006						
Dec.	1	Balance	✓			5 0 0 33
	17	Purchase		2 3 2 1 56		2 8 2 1 89
	8	Payment			5 0 0 33	2 3 2 1 56

ACCOUNT Michelle Weinstein   **ACCOUNT NO.** 2745

DATE		DESCRIPTION	POST REF.	DEBIT	CREDIT	BALANCE
2006						
Dec.	1	Balance	ü			4 8 7 22
	3	payment	SJ35		4 8 7 22	—0—
	11	purchase	SJ35	1 3 2 8 13		1 3 2 8 13

Accounts
Payable Ledger

ACCOUNTS PAYABLE LEDGER
CREDITORS

Archival Card Storage Suppliers
Autograph Central
Bracket Sports Collector
Calderon Sports Supply
Duong's Jersey Outlet
International Sports Supplies
Ringside Entertainment
Sports Authentica
Toy Warehouse
Woodworks, Inc.
Worldwide Tennis

Name_____ Date_____ Class_____

NAME _____ Archival Card Storage Suppliers _____ **TERMS** _____ n/30 _____
ADDRESS _____ 7456 Palace Parkway, Dallas, TX 75201 _____

DATE		DESCRIPTION	POST REF.	DEBIT	CREDIT	BALANCE
2006						
Dec.	1	Balance	✓			6 5 0 00
	1	Payment check# 609		650 00		-0-

NAME _____ Autograph Central _____ **TERMS** _____ 2/10, n/30 _____
ADDRESS _____ 225 Central Expressway #500, Grand Prairie, TX 75050 _____

DATE		DESCRIPTION	POST REF.	DEBIT	CREDIT	BALANCE
2006						
Dec	9	Purchased signed Basketballs			2000 00	2000 00
	15	Payment check #628		1960 00		40 00
		Purchase Discount		40 00		-0-

NAME _____ Bracket Sports Collector _____ **TERMS** _____ n/30 _____
ADDRESS _____ 52127 Fredrick Lane, Suite 200, Mesquite, TX 75149 _____

DATE		DESCRIPTION	POST REF.	DEBIT	CREDIT	BALANCE
2006						
Dec.	1	Balance	✓			1000 00

Name_____ Date_____ Class_____

NAME   Calderon Sports Supply   **TERMS**   5/10, n/30

ADDRESS   1212 Selby Lane, Suite 27, Dallas, TX 75202

DATE		DESCRIPTION	POST REF.	DEBIT	CREDIT	BALANCE
2006						
Dec	11	Purchased die-cast cars			800 00	800 00
	16	Payment check 630		760 00		40 00
		Discount 5%		40 00		0

NAME   Duong's Jersey Outlet   **TERMS**   n/30

ADDRESS   7500 East Park Street, Suite 500, Grand Prairie, TX 75051

DATE		DESCRIPTION	POST REF.	DEBIT	CREDIT	BALANCE
2006						
Dec	3	Purchases			650 00	650 00
	5					

NAME   International Sports Supplies   **TERMS**   2/10, n/310

ADDRESS   492 West Main Street, Grand Prairie, TX 75050

DATE		DESCRIPTION	POST REF.	DEBIT	CREDIT	BALANCE
2006						
Dec.	1	Balance	✓			3 2 0 0 00
	9	Payment		3 1 3 6 00		6 4 00
		Purchase Discount		6 4 00		0
	30	purchase banners and jerseys			1 2 0 0 00	1 2 0 0 00

Home Team Advantage Practice Set

NAME _____Ringside Entertainment_____ **TERMS** __2/10, n/30__

ADDRESS _____99 Klein Parkway, Dallas, TX 75212_____

DATE		DESCRIPTION	POST REF.	DEBIT	CREDIT	BALANCE
2006						
Dec	22	Purchased video tapes			600 00	600 00
	30	payment		600 00		0

NAME _____Sports Authentica_____ **TERMS** __n/30__

ADDRESS _____12472 I-10 West, Suite 700, Houston, TX 75942_____

DATE		DESCRIPTION	POST REF.	DEBIT	CREDIT	BALANCE
2006						
Dec.	1	Balance	✓			500 00
	4	Payment check # 612		500 00		0
	10	purchased Autographed baseballs			1000 00	1000 00
	16	purchased Hockey Pucks			500 00	1500 00
	30	Payment		500 00		1000 00

NAME _____Toy Warehouse_____ **TERMS** __n/30__

ADDRESS _____1250 Farber Avenue, Chicago, IL 60651_____

DATE		DESCRIPTION	POST REF.	DEBIT	CREDIT	BALANCE
2006						
Dec	24	Purchase action figures			2400 00	2400 00

Name_____ Date_____ Class_____

NAME Woodworks, Inc. **TERMS** 2/10, n/30

ADDRESS 5259 Central Parkway, #142, Dallas, TX 75201

DATE		DESCRIPTION	POST REF.	DEBIT	CREDIT	BALANCE
2006						
Dec	3	Bat display cases			750 00	750 00
	8	Payment check #620		735 00		15 00
		Purchase Discount		15 00		0
	11	Purchase die cast car Display			450 00	450 00
	15	Payment check 627		441 00		9 00
		Purchase Discount		9 00		0

NAME Worldwide Tennis **TERMS** 2/10, n/30

ADDRESS 10339 Santa Monica Blvd., Los Angeles, CA 90025

DATE		DESCRIPTION	POST REF.	DEBIT	CREDIT	BALANCE
2006						
Dec	24	Purchased autographed portrait			300 00	300 00

Accounting
Stationery

Home Team Advantage Practice Set

Home Team Advantage
Schedule of Accounts Payable
December 31, 2006

Home Team Advantage
Schedule of Accounts Receivable
December 31, 2006

Terri Alenikou	58 44	
Jeff Briggs	76 50	
Steve Carlyle	3 586 88	
Laurie Chapman	1 542 15	
Wendy Gau	770 31	
Debbie Gutierrez	676 64	
Dave Jordan	1 992 19	
Rick Marquez	437 25	
Monica Mooney	456 88	
Kathy Oh	791 34	
Linda Padilla	4 332 78	
Ann Roff	658 75	
Brad Smythe	2 321 56	
Michelle Weinstein	1 328 13	
Mike Antonello	2 347 97	
Kristen Boucher	665 09	
	19 443 36	271.38

Home Team Advantage Practice Set

Name_____ Date_____ Class_____

Home Team

Work

For the Year

	POST REF.	ACCOUNT NAME	TRIAL BALANCE		ADJUSTMENTS	
			DEBIT	CREDIT	DEBIT	CREDIT
1						
2						
3						
4						
5						
6						
7						
8						
9						
10						
11						
12						
13						
14						
15						
16						
17						
18						
19						
20						
21						
22						
23						
24						
25						
26						
27						
28						
29						
30						
31						
32						
33						
34						
35						
36						
37						
38						
39						

Home Team Advantage Practice Set   Copyright © 2007 The McGraw-Hill Companies

Name_____ Date_____ Class_____

Advantage_____

Sheet_____

Ended December 31, 2006_____

ADJUSTED TRIAL BALANCE		INCOME STATEMENT		BALANCE SHEET		
DEBIT	CREDIT	DEBIT	CREDIT	DEBIT	CREDIT	
						1
						2
						3
						4
						5
						6
						7
						8
						9
						10
						11
						12
						13
						14
						15
						16
						17
						18
						19
						20
						21
						22
						23
						24
						25
						26
						27
						28
						29
						30
						31
						32
						33
						34
						35
						36
						37
						38
						39

Home Team Advantage Practice Set

Name_____ Date_____ Class_____

	POST REF.	ACCOUNT NAME	TRIAL BALANCE		ADJUSTMENTS	
			DEBIT	CREDIT	DEBIT	CREDIT
1						
2						
3						
4						
5						
6						
7						
8						
9						
10						
11						
12						
13						
14						
15						
16						
17						
18						
19						
20						
21						
22						
23						
24						
25						
26						
27						
28						
29						
30						
31						
32						
33						
34						
35						
36						
37						
38						
39						

Home Team Advantage Practice Set

Name_____ Date_____Class_____

Advantage_____

Sheet_____

Ended December 31, 2006_____

ADJUSTED TRIAL BALANCE		INCOME STATEMENT		BALANCE SHEET		
DEBIT	CREDIT	DEBIT	CREDIT	DEBIT	CREDIT	
						1
						2
						3
						4
						5
						6
						7
						8
						9
						10
						11
						12
						13
						14
						15
						16
						17
						18
						19
						20
						21
						22
						23
						24
						25
						26
						27
						28
						29
						30
						31
						32
						33
						34
						35
						36
						37
						38
						39

Home Team Advantage Practice Set

Name_____ Date_____ Class_____

Home Team Advantage

Income Statement

Year Ended December 31, 2006

Home Team Advantage Practice Set

Name_____ Date_____ Class_____

Home Team Advantage
Statement of Owner's Equity
December 31, 2006

Home Team Advantage Practice Set

Name_____ Date_____ Class_____

Home Team Advantage

Balance Sheet

December 31, 2006

Home Team Advantage Practice Set   Copyright © 2007 The McGraw-Hill Companies

Name_____ Date_____ Class_____

<table>
<tr><td colspan="4" align="center">Home Team Advantage</td></tr>
<tr><td colspan="4" align="center">Postclosing Trial Balance</td></tr>
<tr><td colspan="4" align="center">December 31, 2006</td></tr>
</table>

Managerial Analysis Questions

MANAGERIAL ANALYSIS QUESTIONS

(1) Accountants often compare a firm's current assets to its current liabilities in order to assess the ability of the firm to pay its short-term debt. A current ratio (current assets divided by current liabilities) of 2 to 1 or better is usually considered safe. Compute the current ratio of Home Team Advantage for the current and prior year. (Refer to the balance sheet on page 22 for the prior year's data.) Comment on the trend in this ratio at Home Team Advantage. Has the firm's ability to pay its current liabilities as they become due improved or worsened?

(2) There is no provision for income tax shown on the income statements of Home Team Advantage. Why?

(3) What is the advantage to Home Team Advantage of having a separate Purchases Returns and Allowances account rather than crediting returns and allowances to the Purchases account directly?

(4) It is a policy of Home Team Advantage to deposit all cash receipts intact in the bank each day. What are the benefits to Home Team Advantage of such a policy?

(5) Home Team Advantage is currently considering the idea of eliminating its charge accounts and accepting only bank credit cards if a customer wants to buy on credit. What are the advantages of accepting only bank credit cards? The disadvantages?

(6) Accountants often compare the cost of goods sold and the gross profit on sales to net sales when analyzing the income statement. Compute the cost of goods sold percentage (cost of goods sold divided by net sales) and the gross profit percentage (gross profit on sales divided by net sales for the current and prior years. (Refer to the income statement on page 21 for the prior year's data.) What is the significance of these percentages in analyzing the ability of Home Team Advantage to control costs and improve net income?

(7) The inventory turnover represents the time period it takes from the purchase of inventory until its sale. Inventory turnover is calculated by dividing the cost of goods sold by the average inventory. Compute the inventory turnover for Home Team Advantage for the current and prior year. (Refer to the income statement on page 21 for the prior year's data.) Comment on the trend in this ratio for Home Team Advantage.

(8) Home Team Advantage has a policy of placing excess cash in short-tem investments such as certificates of deposit and U.S. Treasury notes. What is the advantage of this policy? What care must be taken in carrying out such a policy?

(9) During the current year, what was the total cost to Home Team Advantage of the employees on its payroll?

(10) What are the advantages of Home Team Advantage having an outside payroll service company prepare its payroll records, checks, and tax returns? What are the disadvantages?

Audit Test

Home Team Advantage Practice Set